D1073646

"Food and faith link you to your heritage. Ethel Hofman's fine story-telling captures the inspiring essence of her mother's inner strength and conviction throughout her lifelong journey."

—*Flo Braker, author,* The Simple Art of Perfect Baking

"Ethel Hofman's **Mackerel at Midnight: Growing Up Jewish on a Remote Scottish Island** is a warm and exciting ethnographic journey. . . . much more than a cookbook and a genuine pleasure to read. A unique insight into Jewish life and foodways."

—*Chef Fritz Blank, Deux Cheminées, Philadelphia*

"**Mackerel at Midnight** is a warm, passionate account of Jewish custom and ritual that blends culture, tradition, and good food in a most unlikely setting. A worthwhile read for the original recipes alone."

—*Menachem Y. Lubinsky, president & CEO,*
LUBICOM Marketing Consulting, New York

"In this gentle and engaging memoir and cookbook, Ethel Hofman tells a tale of the Shetland Islands from the unusual perspective of a lone Jewish family living in this distant outpost of Scotland in the 1900s. . . . In a world growing increasingly uncertain the preservation of tradition becomes even more critical. From that perspective, **Mackerel at Midnight** makes a distinctive contribution, giving us a memorable portrait of a way of life that was and, lamentably, is no more."

—*Cara De Silva, writer and editor*, In Memory's Kitchen:
A legacy from the Women of Terezin

"In this charming, heart-warming, touching, and delicious memoir of a family's devotions to Yiddishkeit in an unbelievably remote and isolated corner of the world, Ethel Hofman, renowned for her culinary creativity, presents the world in which she grew up in a tale that you won't be able to put down."

—*Myra Chanin, food editor,* Elements Magazine

"A fascinating, real-life account of a Jewish family in the Christian Shetland Islands. With pride in both her Jewish and Scottish heritage, Hofman combines the story of her life in the remote Shetland Islands with recipes I can't wait to try. An engaging read."

—*Caroline Orzes, editor and publisher,*
Jewish Life & Style, Las Vegas

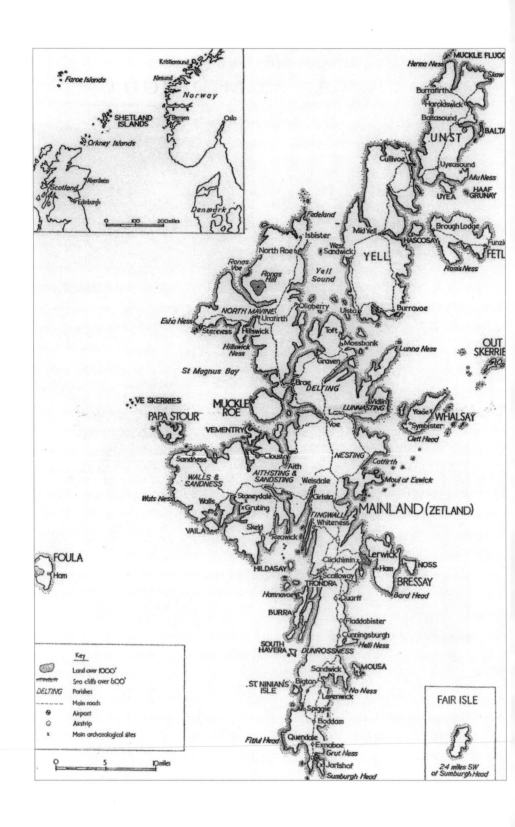

*To Sheila
Warmest wishes
Ethel G. Hofman*

MACKEREL AT MIDNIGHT

Growing Up Jewish on a Remote Scottish Island

ETHEL G. HOFMAN

"If you wish to give a gift which is
truly forever, give memories."
Rabbi Abraham J. Twerski, M.D.

Small boat harbor, Lerwick. *Courtesy of* The Shetland Times, *Lerwick*

Camino Books, Inc.
Philadelphia

Copyright © 2005 by Ethel G. Hofman
All Rights Reserved

No part of this book may be reproduced in any form or by any electronic or mechanical means including information storage and retrieval systems without permission in writing from the publisher, except by a reviewer who may quote brief passages in a review.

Manufactured in the United States of America

1 2 3 4 5 08 07 06 05

Library of Congress Cataloging-in-Publication Data

Hofman, Ethel G., 1939-
    Mackerel at midnight : growing up Jewish on a remote Scottish island / by Ethel G. Hofman.
    p. cm.
    ISBN 0-940159-93-7 (alk. paper)
1. Cookery, Jewish. I. Title.

TX724.H64 2005
641.5'676—dc22   2004023648

Cover and interior design: Jerilyn Bockorick
Cover photograph: *Simmer dim*, summer midnight at Hamnavoe pier.
    Courtesy of Dr. Walter I. Hofman.
Frontispiece: Map of Shetland Islands, from James R. Nicolson, *Shetland* (Devon, England: David and Charles, Ltd., 1972). Courtesy of the author.

This book is available at a special discount on bulk purchases for promotional, business, and educational use.

Publisher
Camino Books, Inc.
P.O. Box 59026
Philadelphia, PA 19102

www.caminobooks.com

In Memory of
Jean and Harry Greenwald
"Our Ma and Dad"

They overcame isolation and cultural barriers to raise their children, Ethel, Roy, and Jack, in the only Jewish family in the Shetland Islands. By their loving example, they instilled in us an intense pride in our Jewish heritage and identity.

May their precious legacy continue for generations to come.

Table of Contents

Acknowledgments

My love and thanks to my dear husband, Walter, a constant source of strength and support. He has always encouraged me to "go one step further," especially in the long process of researching and writing this book. After more than forty years, he is still happily reading manuscripts (when asked), as well as testing the recipes, tasting the results, and vigorously scrubbing the mountains of pots and pans in the kitchen sink. In self-defense, he has come into his own as a recognized barbecue maven.

To my brother, Roy Greenwald, who searched the Shetland archives, reminded me of countless forgotten anecdotes, and passed on stories and old letters relating to the Greenwalds' early years in Shetland. We laughed and cried and treasure each memory.

To my brother Jack Greenwald, in reply to "why don't I ever get mentioned?" You were born long after Roy and I were a team, but your family support and daily reminders of Ma's humor are lovingly appreciated.

To Lewis and Sylvette Greenwald, who spent long hours on the Internet to come up with information on the Gorodea *shtetl* and who provided generational facts and long-lost family photographs. You're terrific.

To John A. Gurski, who was on call any time of the day or night to walk me through my computer glitches, and John Jr., who painstakingly wrote it all down, step by step, so that a computer illiterate like me could understand. My grateful thanks.

To Ken Bookman, who gave freely of editorial advice and let me unwind over numerous cups of fresh-brewed coffee, in return for a bagel and cream cheese, "plain please."

To Jerry Etter, who jumped in to help edit when I was desperate. You had the patience and good nature to decode my writing, time and time again. But for you, I'd still be struggling.

Special thanks to Vaila Wishart, editor of *The Shetland Times*, and Dennis Coutts, of Lerwick, for permission to use photographs; and to Brian Smith of the Shetland archives, for his patience and help in perusing original documents.

To Rebe Pearson and Charlie and Jim Laurenson for allowing me the use of the Laurenson family names. The shared stories, tea, and *bannocks* in Rebe's cozy kitchen in the Glen remain treasured memories.

Sincere thanks to James R. Nicolson—who, as the publisher of *Shetland Life* magazine, accepted my first articles on the Greenwalds for publication—for permission to use the map of Shetland as it appears in his book *Shetland* (Devon, England: David and Charles, Ltd., 1972).

To Myra Chanin, who, with humor, logic, and insight, set me on the right path to write about growing up Jewish in Shetland. Myra, you understood. You've been there.

Though the photographs in this book are from the Greenwald family collection, duplicates of several are available in the Shetland Museum Photographic Archives. Special thanks to them for gathering a fascinating anthology of "old Shetland."

And to all my friends in Shetland who shared recipes and regaled me with their memories of the "Greenvalds," who came to the islands in the early twentieth century, my sincere thanks and appreciation.

Sincere thanks also to Barbara Gibbons, for her endless patience and invaluable editing expertise, and to Edward Jutkowitz, who had enough faith in me and fascination with my story to publish this book.

Note to the Reader

Many years have elapsed since these events took place. The stories in this book are based on the sometimes conflicting recollections of many people. To prevent any unintentional misrepresentation or embarrassment, I have changed certain names, and, in some cases, places and times.

Introduction

Jean Segal Greenwald, my mother, was a remarkable woman. You, the reader, never met her, but the story of how she raised a Jewish family far away from the support of a Jewish community will move and inspire you.

She told me her story in snatches over the years. As I was growing up, my mother talked of my grandmother, whose hardships in some ways paralleled her own, though both women did not share the same experience of alienation in a strange land. Through her perseverance, however, my mother overcame adversity, so that eventually she enjoyed a comfortable, rewarding life. Later, on my frequent visits "home" and on her extended visits to me in the United States, her memories would come up in casual conversations. Without realizing it, I gained a vivid picture of her struggles and her family life.

She was "our Ma." Her deep faith never faltered, even under the most stressful circumstances—too numerous to count. She had a staunch inner strength, which gave her the ability to rise above the grief and obstacles she encountered in her unique daily life: growing up in the Glasgow Gorbals, and her gripping experiences as a young bride adapting to a Christian community on a remote island, completely separated from the familiar culture she had grown up with.

My mother arrived in Shetland in April 1935, newly wed to a husband she barely knew. He had fled from the brutality of pogroms and harsh life in a Russian *shtetl*; she had grown up in Scotland in a poor but observant Jewish family of Lithuanian descent. Theirs was a marriage of convenience, a loveless union arranged by the *shadchen*. Her husband brought her across the Atlantic Ocean to live in the midst of a Christian community, with one hundred churches and halls where a devout Christian population worshipped, but with no rabbi, no synagogue—none of the support systems of Jewish life.

For Ma, assimilating would have been the easiest thing to do; she could have cast aside her Jewish values and tradition and silently blended into the Christian community. But she was determined to retain her religion and culture. By her example, she instilled high moral values and a profound Jewish identity in my brothers and me—an amazing accomplishment. Trying to put myself in her place, I wonder if I could have had the courage and determination to hold fast to my Judaism. As I grow older, I realize the enormity of her daily struggles to adapt, while maintaining her Jewish beliefs without the benefit of family close by.

As a child, I dearly wanted to grow up and do all the things I saw my mother doing and admired her for. As a wife and mother, I find myself emulating her in a hundred ways. When I try on a dress, I hear her brisk voice over my shoulder: "Take it off. It doesn't do a thing for you." And I do. Or, as I take a cake from the oven, her approval comes through in a soft whisper, with a hint of dialect, "isn't that chust lovely," and I blush from her praise.

But, above all, she was dedicated to raising me and my two brothers as Jews, with pride in our culture and the practice of our religion, although we were more than two hundred miles across an ocean from the nearest Jewish community.

For Ma, cooking for family and neighbors was therapeutic. It was an infallible cure for the occasional bouts of loneliness and feelings of separation from other Jews. In winter, we'd come home to a plate of steaming ruby-red borscht, thick with grated fresh beets "to warm the cockles of your heart." In warm weather, we cooled off with a glass of tangy schav, a drink made from the wild sorrel that grew along country paths.

Included in this collection of stories from a quieter, gentler era are some of my favorite island recipes—slightly updated in order to fit in with today's lifestyles and contemporary kitchen appliances—simple, wholesome recipes "made with love."

I am eternally grateful for Ma's example, her morals, her values, and motivation. Her precious gift to her children was a passport to a rich, fulfilling, and meaningful future.

1

Our Ma

Growing up in Lerwick, in the Shetlands, other children had Mother or Mummy, but not the Greenwald kids. We had "our Ma."

She would tell us that in the tenements of Glasgow, where she grew up, every mother was Ma. "If she was Mother or Mummy," she explained, "you were looked on as toffee-nosed, above your station, trying to be like the genteel folk you were not."

So, Ma it was. We were comfortable with it and so was she.

As a child, she was Jean Segal, the youngest of three daughters. She and her sisters, Rosie and Sadie, lived on the top floor of an overcrowded tenement in the Glasgow Gorbals with their parents, Jacob and Esther. Picture New York's Lower East Side, in the early 1900s, where thousands of European immigrants packed the streets and tenements, and you have the Glasgow Gorbals, though on a smaller scale. It was an area swarming with pushcarts, peddlers, and families living in cramped conditions and trying to eke out a living in a "free country."

Jacob and Esther Segal had left Lithuania with a wave of immigrants in the late 1800s. They disembarked in Greenock, the Glasgow seaport, in search of safety and prosperity. They found safety but, sadly, not the prosperity they had hoped for. Ma sighed. "Your grandmother was a fine seamstress, and that's what kept the family together. In Lithuania, your grandfather was a tailor, but he was ill with diabetes, increasingly so, and we couldn't afford the insulin which would have kept him alive. And as if that wasn't enough, our little four-year-old brother died of meningitis." My grandmother, Esther, never recovered from the heartbreak.

Our Ma, at Andy's Bar mitzvah

Ma, her black, curly hair now streaked with gray, leaned back in her favorite armchair, looking out onto the harbor she had sailed into more than sixty years ago. "Never in my wildest dreams did I imagine that I would spend my life in these isles. But then I thought that getting married would let me escape from Glasgow."

I listened, holding onto every word. "Was life so terrible?"

"It was hard. Remember, my parents came with very little money, had to learn English, and jobs were scarce. My mother could hardly make ends meet. There was barely enough money to live on."

"How did she manage to feed the family?"

"She found out that, at the end of the day, the vendors gave away overripe fruit and vegetables. So at four o'clock in the afternoon, she walked to the marketplace, an empty basket over her arm and a few pennies in her pocket. The vendors knew her. I suppose they felt sorry for her. She had a sick husband and three young children to feed. They would keep something back if she was late. At the fishmonger's, she got scraps of herring and fish, and, from the butcher, she would get some marrowbones. With the little she had, she could make a filling meal, so we rarely went hungry."

Looking at Ma, I could see in her eyes sad memories now mellowed by time. "Your grandmother was an exceptional cook," she smiled. "And you're just like her."

This is an inheritance of which I'm fiercely proud.

For the Gorbals girls, school came to an end when they turned fourteen and had to go to work. Every family needed the extra *pay packet*. The Segals were no different. Ma had graduated at the top of her class in school and at *cheder*. In the bedroom she shared with her sisters, she wept bitterly.

"I don't want to leave school. I love it." What could she do? "Maybe I could be a hairdresser," she thought. "After all, I cut and set Sadie's hair all the time and I'm good at it."

"Talk to Ma," suggested Sadie, without much enthusiasm. She wasn't interested in her sister's problems. She had already applied for a visa and affidavits from a distant relative in Canada. "As soon as I have all the documents, I'll be leaving."

Ma ran into the kitchen. Her mother was sitting at the table, head in hands, the picture of weariness.

"I want to go to hairdressing school," she announced.

"You know you have to pay, and we just don't have the money."

Grandma Esther, *left*, and friend

Esther thought hard. "Go and get dressed in your smartest outfit," she ordered. "We're going to your uncle's house."

Uncle Maury had arrived with the first wave of immigrants a decade before. He quickly became well established in the Glasgow business world. Ma expressed his rapid rise thus: "He now has money in his pocket."

Esther was not proud when it came to asking for help for her children. She was a progressive thinker. "Education is the only way out of a life of drudgery, even for a girl." Those were the days when a girl was expected to get married to a husband who would provide for her.

The next day, mother and daughter, both dressed in threadbare but spotlessly clean outfits, took a bus out of the congested Gorbals to Pollockshields, the wealthy part of town. A butler led them into an overdecorated Victorian parlor to wait. There was no welcome. Ma remembers, "We weren't even offered a cup of tea." Esther pleaded with Uncle Maury.

"You know that the children can't get anywhere without an education. Jean is very clever and wants to be a hairdresser so she can make something of herself. We can't afford the money for her to apprentice. Can you help?"

They were shown out, his scathing answer ringing in their ears. "There are no handouts here! Let her get a job."

Hiding her tears, Esther forced herself to speak harshly. "You have to find work. There's no choice." The family had sold whatever valuable items they possessed, including a brass samovar and silver bowls, to the Glasgow museum, the People's Palace. Sadly, there could be no further discussion. Ma needed a job. A career was impossible.

Back in the Gorbals, they pushed their way through the noisy, crowded streets, past the carts loaded with fruit, vegetables, and used clothing, and climbed the stairs to the dingy two-room apartment. Devastated, Ma sobbed herself into a fitful sleep, dreaming of lost opportunity.

But Ma had inherited the genes of a survivor, along with a good helping of *chutzpah*, attributes that would stand her in good stead throughout her life. She was not about to scrub steps or clean houses for "the gentry." The next day, she took two buses out of the Gorbals to Gerber's, a high-fashion women's clothing store in the center of Glasgow.

"I'd like to talk with the manager."

"What do you want with the manager?" asked the saleslady sternly, eyeing the unsophisticated young woman up and down. "She doesn't usually come out onto the floor."

Ma met her gaze unflinchingly. "I need a job and I'll do anything."

A tall, forbidding, poker-faced manager, dressed from head to toe in starched black gabardine, marched out from behind a curtained

The Segal women, *left to right*, Jean, Mother Esther, and Sadie

alcove. She looked at Ma with disdain, ready to dismiss this young up-start. But perhaps Ma's candor and stylish appearance impressed her. Hat and gloves and shoes were perfectly matched. The shoes were polished to a high gloss and the silver buckles sparkled. Though Ma's coat was frayed at the cuffs, it was clean and neatly pressed. The man-ager decided to make an exception. "I only employ women with experience, but you can have a job as a go-fer. We'll try you out for a week and see how you do," she said.

Rules were strict and to be followed to the letter. "Run errands, make tea for the tea break, stay out of the salesgirls' way, and only help if asked. Whenever Mr. Gerber rings for his tea, get it promptly. Bring it to his office on a tray, with a white napkin folded just so, and arrange two chocolate biscuits, side by side, on a plate with a *d'oyley*."

Ma conducted herself with as much decorum as her enthusiasm would allow. She couldn't afford to lose this job. She closely observed the interaction between the salesladies and customers. When the saleswomen recognized her extraordinary capacity for coordinating stylish outfits, they constantly beckoned her to the floor for suggestions. Within a few months, her talents elevated her to the status of salesgirl.

She never tired of boasting. "I have a keen eye for fashion. And it was easy to dress each woman according to her personality and build. In fact, you could say I was the initiator of mix and match." She built up a clientele of women who demanded that Ma wait on them or they would walk out of the store. "Real *toffs* they were. I dressed them from head to toe, from hat to shoes. They could afford expensive clothes, but they didn't have my good taste. They went out of the shop thrilled to bits, outfitted by Jean." She chuckled at the memory. "I could even make an ugly duckling look good."

The weekly pay, a few shillings, was handed over to a grateful Esther. The extra money meant that she didn't have to sew late into the night; there was more food on the table, and, occasionally, the whole family had new clothes. Ma received one shilling a week for bus fare and entertainment.

"I was happy to get it," Ma recalled. "That's just what you had to do. But we had good times. It wasn't all dreary. For sixpence we could go to the Locarno dance hall on a Saturday night. You never knew who you might meet. On a Saturday, Sadie, Rosie, and I would go to Lewis's department store. I loved trying on hats that we couldn't afford to buy. Every hat I tried on looked great. On my sisters they looked ridiculous, which led to tremendous jealousy." In Shetland, when Ma wasn't wearing a woolen hat to keep warm, she walked down the main street, stylish in a wide-brimmed hat.

Ma worked at Gerbers until she was twenty-five. Her friends were already married with babies. Although they were all toiling in the tenements, trying to make ends meet, they looked on Ma with pity. "She's an old maid, left on the shelf."

That bothered and saddened her. "I wanted to have a husband, a home and family, but nobody wanted a woman without a *nedan*. The young Glasgow men were just not interested, no matter that I was outgoing, and, though I say it myself, I was damned attractive."

At dances or on walks in the park, there was always the chance and hope of "meeting the man of my dreams." However, the pickings were slim to nonexistent. As a last resort, there was the *shadchen*. That was how Jean met and married Harry.

2

Pochapovsky to Greenwald: From Russia to Shetland

It was almost a century ago when Harry landed in Lerwick, Shetland, with his father, Louis, and brothers, Hyman and Woolf. The Pochapovsky family had struggled trying to earn a living in Gorodea, a Belarussian *shtetl* near Minsk, where the population was made up of 688 Jews and a few Gentiles.

For the Jews, life was fraught with fear, danger, and persecution. As the Cossacks rode in on horseback, with whips lashing out and wild shouts of "beat the Jews!" families fled to hide behind barred doors. Anyone left outside, be it man, woman, or child, was certain to be badly injured. Until the Cossacks rode away, the Jews might be left to die in the street. Jewish men faced a twenty-five-year conscription into the Czarist army. At the end of that time, those who had left their homes young and vibrant would return old and broken. Little wonder that Harry buried these ghoulish memories—so painful that he never ever talked about his childhood—deep into his soul.

The Pochapovsky men decided, "There's no choice. It will be a long, hard journey, but we have to leave." They had no close ties to the *shtetl*. Louis was a widower and his sons, unmarried. "We'll sell everything. Then we should have enough to purchase passage on a ship bound for the Golden Medinah." Rumors had reached the *shtetls* that in America the streets were paved with gold.

"We must change our name. It's too Russian," said Hyman, the quiet one. Trekking through Germany, they became the Greenwalds. It was the custom to buy a new name from some impoverished family, happy to exchange names for a few rubles.

In France, they stayed long enough to learn some rudimentary

Dad in World War I uniform

French. Finally, they arrived at the port of Le Havre. On the dock, Louis pushed his way through the human mass of men, women, and children, all clutching their belongings in battered boxes and baskets. At the makeshift ticket office, he carefully counted out some notes and two gold sovereigns.

"Four tickets to America," he requested in broken English," adding, "in steerage."

The ticketmaster sneered. "You'll be lucky to get a space on the deck. The ship is loaded to the gunwales. There's not a bunk to be had."

"I've come a long way. We've traveled for weeks. We'll take anything as long as we get on board," he pleaded.

The ticketmaster yielded, thinking they would find themselves a corner somewhere on the deck.

They exchanged money and tickets. Finally, on board, pushing their way to a vacant space, the Greenwald men looked at each other triumphantly as the French shore slid into the mists and out of sight. "We're on our way."

Hours later the loudspeaker blared, "Everybody off for America, everybody off—America."

There were questions in Yiddish. "We're there already?" No one paid attention.

The passengers recognized the one word *America*. Jubilant, they rushed down the gangplank onto the dock, where people were milling around.

Frantically, the Greenwald men, bags on their backs, pushed their way from the dockside through the hordes of people. Abruptly, joy was replaced by confusion. This destination was cold, dark, and eerie.

"Is this America?" they asked each other. Passing by, a drunken sailor leered—"You're in the port of Greenock." This inhospitable town was the seaport outside of Glasgow, Scotland.

Hundreds of tricked European immigrants now gathered, disappointed and angry, waving fists at the ship that had pulled speedily away from the dock, sailing down the river Clyde towards the ocean. Too late. Stunned, they realized the ship's captain had cheated them. The story goes that in order to pocket double fares he took advantage of the passengers' lack of English and then took on a new batch of passengers.

Standing in predawn darkness, with grim, granite buildings looming on both sides of rain-slicked streets, Harry cursed in Yiddish.

"What a *gonif* is the captain. This is not the Golden Medinah; it's a lousy, cold place. Maybe we should have stayed in the old country."

Louis stared at his son in astonishment. "You want to go back and be killed, or, worse, maimed by the Cossacks? Don't be a fool. We're going on."

"But we don't have enough money for another fare."

After heated argument, they came to a joint agreement.

"We'll go no further. We will find work, we will save, and we will go to America."

New immigrants swarmed all over Glasgow, most of them settling in the Gorbals, where two or three families apiece crowded into small apartments, and carts selling everything from pickles to yard goods lined the street. Jobs were scarce. With their Yiddish–English, few skills, and pennilessness, the majority became peddlers wandering from city to town, striving to sell a motley assortment of needles, thread, and ribbons. These homeless men and women rarely strayed into the countryside, where houses might be miles apart.

The Greenwald men were different. Spunky and adventurous, they decided to venture further. "We have no families to support. Let's get away from Glasgow and get away from these *gonifs*."

"Fine. But we must deal in something other than *tchotchkes* or we'll never make it," said Woolf, a progressive businessman.

They bartered a few pieces of jewelry for work. At a pawnshop, they bought a brown leather case lined in blue velvet, with a strong gold lock and key. That case, almost a hundred years old now, has survived to become a family heirloom.

At night, in their shabby room in a dockside boarding house, the men pored over a dog-eared map of Scotland. The Shetland Islands were tucked into a square at the top left-hand corner. The page wasn't long enough to insert the islands, which are on latitude 60 degrees north, level with the southern tip of Greenland.

It was unanimous. "That's where we'll go. It will be an adventure." Excited at the prospect, they set out on foot, trudging along dirt roads north to Aberdeen. Occasionally they would get a lift from a wagon going between farms. But no one they met was interested in buying jewelry. Aberdonians have the reputation of being tight with money, and most everyone they met had the same line: "We don't have money . . . we barter for food. Jewelry is for the wealthy who live in the big houses."

Harry was despondent. "I hope we have better luck soon. We're almost down to our last kopek." He still thought in Russian currency.

"Don't worry," assured Woolf. "I'll think of something."

Louis smiled, albeit sadly. He had a secret. Nine gold sovereigns were hidden in a pouch around his neck under his woolen shirt. He was comforted by "my security."

They made it to the Aberdeen dockyards. The hulking black ship SS *St. Magnus*, which sailed between Aberdeen and Shetland with a stop at the Orkney Islands, was tied up to the pier. A fishy smell, which still hangs over the dockyards, was so pungent even the north

Lodberry, a smuggler's haven

wind couldn't blow it away. Fishing boats had been stranded for days in the harbor, unable to battle the Force 9 (90-mile-an-hour) gales blowing in from the north.

An old, gray-haired man, muffled up to the ears in thick tweeds and layered with yellow oilskins, was leaning against the esplanade wall, sheltered from the wind.

"Where does the boat go?" Harry asked.

"Not going anywhere in this storm," replied the man. Noting Harry's unusual dress, black breeches and long coat, he was curious. "Where do you come from?"

"Far away. My homeland is a poor, cold, and dangerous country—we had to leave."

Feeling sorry for these foreigners, the old man elaborated. "Well, when the wind dies down, that boat goes up north to the Shetland Islands. It's a rough crossing, about fourteen hours. The only folk there are fishermen and *crofters*. It's pretty desolate."

"Any shops?"

"One or two in Lerwick. That's where we dock and unload."

Harry chuckled, something he hadn't done in a long time. "No competition. That's the place we should travel to."

They bought the cheapest steerage tickets and boarded, along with a cargo of stinking, mewling sheep and cows. Their shipboard companions were a score of boisterous whalers who couldn't wait to get home to their wives and sweethearts after a lonely year fishing in the South Shetland Isles, even less populated and more desolate than the North Shetland Isles.

In the grey light of dawn, the *St. Magnus* slid into Lerwick harbor. Husky, bearded men, hauled on thick, steel ropes as the massive ship slowly rode over heaving waves to dock at Victoria Pier. Along the shore, the furious sea lashed against stone buildings that seemed hunched like old women, shrouded in a raw, gauzy drizzle. Low doors, dark holes in the walls, marked the entrances to the *lodberries*, sea-level cellars where, in the late nineteenth century, smugglers had stashed contraband whisky, gin, and tobacco. Lerwick was deserted. A thin light was breaking through a heavy cloud cover, but not a soul was in sight.

Harry stood on deck, staring. "What have we come to now? What kind of people are here?"

Taking charge, he quickly pulled himself together. "We've arrived at our destination. Now, we must find a place to live."

Gathering their battered suitcases and the precious jewelry box, Louis, Harry, Woolf, and Hyman tramped down the rickety gangplank into a strange new life.

3

Strangers and Foreigners

In 1918, arriving in Lerwick from Scotland, the Greenwalds were in completely unfamiliar territory. Although they may have picked up some Gaelic on their travels through the Scottish mainland, they found little or no Scottish culture in Shetland. There is no clan system there and Shetlanders do not speak Gaelic. History and present-day customs are steeped in Norse and Scandinavian culture. The Norsemen, who called the islands Hjaltland, had settled peacefully in Shetland between the eighth and eleventh centuries.

Of the more than one hundred Shetland Islands, only seventeen are inhabited, but the Viking and Norse influences are evident everywhere, from the capital town of Lerwick to outlying islands such as Fetlar, Papa Stour, and Unst. Ancient sites such as Jarlshof and Mousa Broch, as well as Norse graves, give archaeologists a clear and fascinating picture of the islands' social history. Modern parishes have been divided according to the Old Norse methods. Place names also derive from the Old Norse, such as Northmavine, meaning "North of the narrow isthmus," where a narrow strip of land divides the North Sea and the Atlantic Ocean. One can stand on the isthmus, and, a few yards to either side, the sea and ocean lap up against the rocky shoreline. Family names like Inkster and Isbister are rooted in Norse, and although English is the official language in schools, the soft, melodious dialect, a combination of Lowland Scots and ancient Norse, is still spoken throughout the islands.

In Shetland, a person can never be more than three miles from the seashore; so Shetlanders have been called "fishermen with a *croft*," through the centuries making a living from both fishing and farming. This changed in the early 1970s, however, with the discovery of oil in the North Sea. Islanders were paid huge salaries to work on the oil rigs. To supplement the work force, men and their families came from the mainland of Scotland and England. Many of these people stayed and are working hard to preserve the islands' heritage and culture.

In the 1920s, Shetlanders were accustomed to the strange language and garb of German and Dutch fishermen on Lerwick's main thoroughfare, Commercial Street. The sheltered stretch of water between Lerwick and the island of Bressay has created one of the best and safest harbors in Britain, and, in summertime, so many fishing boats were anchored in Bressay Sound that, Ma recalled, "You could walk from boat to boat, from Lerwick until you were almost at the Bressay pier."

Harry, Hyman, and Woolf had shaved off their beards, but, like their father, Louis, they still wore the long black coats and thick-soled, laced ankle-boots, the dress of the Russian peasants. They walked slowly along Commercial Street. The north end of the cobbled street snaked around and under the shadow of Fort Charlotte, a fortification built in 1643 by Oliver Cromwell. Now and again, on their way, searching for a place to live, the Greenwalds paused to look in the windows of the few shops, Woolf happily noting, "There are no jewelers in this town."

Renting an apartment was easy. A shrewd landlord, however, realizing that the foreigners had only a smattering of English and little understanding of the Shetland dialect, doubled the rental price. Checking the archives, we found that Louis Greenwald paid sixteen pounds sterling, the rent for one year. Other entries for apartments in the same building noted rents of half that amount.

But they had a roof over their heads and fish was cheap. "And it's not cold, like in Gorodea," Louis told his sons. "And best of all, we don't have to be afraid for our lives." The Shetland Islands, warmed by the Gulf Stream, has a temperate climate, hovering around forty degrees in the winter and the mid-sixties in summer.

At first the local people were suspicious. "Who are these strangers who have come among us?" they whispered to each other. Shetlanders had never heard such a strange language or seen Jews and such foreign dress before. But the Greenwalds were smart. They quickly picked up the Shetland dialect, gave it a smattering of Yiddish, and donned the standard fishermen's wear of heavy trousers and knitted sweaters. Once the Lerwegians got to know Louis and his sons, they accepted and even welcomed them. Neighbors explained, "We just read about you in the

Bible. The good book says the Jews are the Chosen People." It became much easier to travel and do business with the islanders.

Travel and rent, paid for a year in advance, had used up almost all of the Greenwalds' money. They needed to make a living, and fast. Louis had seen some third- or fourth-hand bicycles propped against the door of the butcher shop, just below their apartment. "We must invest in bicycles. We'll be able to travel further," he told his sons.

News travels fast in a small community. The morning after they had moved in, the butcher, a ruddy-cheeked, stocky gentleman, knocked on their door. "I hear you wanted some bikes. Maybe you can use a motorbike. It's in good fettle, but occasionally you might have to stop and pump up the tires." After a bit of bargaining and a trial run along the street, the Greenwalds agreed to buy it. They soon found out that "good fettle" was somewhat of an overstatement. The tires constantly leaked air. Hyman insisted, "I'll use it. It's still better than going on foot." Meantime, Harry and Woolf had acquired two bicycles, rationalizing, "no need for petrol." In spite of breakdowns, the men could reach some of the most remote areas. They brought jewelry most islanders had never seen except in books. The late Johann Laurenson marveled, "When

Uncle Hyman on his newly acquired motorbike, 1920

Harry came, it was just like Christmas. He had so many *bonnie* things to show us."

The men branched out to cover separate areas. Harry's visits were social occasions. He was outgoing and always had a joke to tell, even if, at first, he was the only one who got it. The *crofters* and fishermen, many of whom lived miles apart, welcomed him. In the land of the midnight sun—*simmer dim*—the islanders could see Harry approaching from a mile away. Quickly, they filled the cast iron kettle—crusted with years of accumulated peat smoke—with water and hung it back on the hook over the open fire, "so Harry can have a cup of hot tea when he gets here." In winter, when darkness falls in early afternoon, he could always be sure of a warm meal and bed for the night. "I'm the postman bringing you news from the metropolis [Lerwick] and messages from your mother," he chuckled as the host family gathered around the glowing peat fire, hanging on to his every word—recognizable, albeit muddled.

The American dream was forgotten. In 1926, the four men pooled their money and bought the building at 163 Commercial Street. At first, it was operated as an ice cream saloon, selling ice cream and *sweeties,* then as a jeweler and watch repair shop.

The first Greenwald shop, early 1920s

But Hyman, Woolf, and their father were tired of the isolation. Woolf had married Sadie Ettinger. Their first baby died ten days after birth and is buried on a hill in the Lerwick cemetery. After the birth of their second baby in Glasgow, Sadie refused to go back to Lerwick. "You can come back to Glasgow or not; it's your choice," she wrote to her husband Woolf. "But I'm staying here in civilization with my own

Uncle Woolf's first advertisement, early 1920s

folk." Harry bought the shop. The rest of the Greenwalds left the island to settle in Glasgow, never to return to Shetland.

By 1934, Harry was well settled and happy with the island life, but he wanted a Jewish wife.

Please Read This.

W. GREENVALD,

JEWELLER, LERWICK,

Is not exaggerating when he says that you cannot get better value anywhere than at his establishment.

As he has been 15 years in the trade, he thoroughly understands it, and can therefore use his knowledge to your advantage.

His Warehouse contains

PRACTICALLY EVERYTHING IMAGINABLE IN JEWELLERY,

and as he is directly connected with Gold and Silversmiths of standing in the South, no order is beyond his execution.

Since coming to this locality, he has won the confidence and esteemed patronage of many Customers through Straight Dealing and First-Class Goods. If you doubt it, or if you don't, give him a trial.

Among the numerous goods in stock are:—

LADIES' AND GENT.'S WALTHAM AND ELGIN WATCHES; GOLD AND SILVER EXPANDING WATCHES; ENGAGEMENT, DRESS, WEDDING, AND SIGNET RINGS; NECKTETS; BROOCHES; CHAINS, AND ALL NOVELTIES; ELECTRO PLATE GOODS IN LARGE VARIETY; SOCIETY BADGES; GOLD AND SILVER CIGARETTE CASES, ETC.

CATALOGUE MAY BE HAD ON APPLICATION.

NOTE NEW ADDRESS—

W. GREENVALD,

THE VARIETY JEWELLER,

163 COMMERCIAL STREET, LERWICK.

PRACTICAL WATCHMAKER KEPT.

ALL REPAIRS PROMPTLY ATTENDED TO.

Shetland Almanac advertisement, 1923

"I'm going to contact Mrs. Goldsmith, the *shadchen* in Glasgow," he thought. "A lot of Jews got off the boat with us and stayed there."

His brothers scoffed when he wrote and told them of his plans for marriage. "What do you need a wife for?" they wrote back. "You have plenty to eat, a roof over your head, and can go wherever you want."

But Harry was adamant. With marriage in mind, he moved into the apartment above the shop at 163 Commercial Street. He wrote to Mrs. Goldsmith, "I want to find a Jewish wife. She must be young, strong, and agreeable to living in the country. P.S., she doesn't have to bring a *nedan*, and I'm well settled."

Mrs. Goldsmith, a widow, was a friend of the Segals. She lived in a tenement in the next street and made a living from arranging marriages, the early twentieth-century version of J-date, the Internet Jewish dating service. She had been unable to marry off the poor Segal sisters. They could bring nothing monetary to a marriage. She rushed as fast as her corseted bulk could to the Segal apartment.

"Jean, I have just the man for you," she said as soon as she could catch her breath. "A fine man, he has a shop and doesn't want a *nedan*. He is very well off. I'm sure he'll give you a good, comfortable home. Will you meet with him?"

Jean hesitated only for a moment, then agreed. This would be an escape from the drudgery of the Gorbals. She was unaware that Mrs. Goldsmith had neglected to mention his age, fifteen years older than Jean, and that his home and business were on a sparsely populated island in the middle of the Atlantic Ocean.

Mail to Shetland was slow. Many weeks later, Harry received descriptions and pictures of two women. One was bordering on fat and had a scarred face that even a photograph couldn't hide. Jean was slender, with curly hair and a winning smile. According to the *shadchen*, "Jean has a beautiful, outgoing personality . . . but, poor as a church mouse."

There was no contest. Harry was bent on meeting Jean. He immediately closed the shop, packed his one suit, and set off on the long journey by boat and train for Glasgow.

Jean agonized over the first meeting. "What shall I wear? Can I straighten my hair? Should I wear lipstick or is it too sluttish? I wonder if he's handsome. Will he like me?"

Her sister Sadie wasn't much help. She was waiting for the affidavit from uncles in America. But Rosie was sympathetic and comforting. "If he doesn't fall madly in love with you, he's crazy. Don't worry, be yourself."

Harry climbed the four flights of steep stone steps to the Segal flat. The building was overcrowded, smoky, and noisy. From each apartment, children's wails and smells of garlic and stale oil floated into the hallway. "She should be happy to get away from this," he thought. "I forgot about the city dirt and squalor. Back in Lerwick, the very air and water are clean. Now I must make an impression on this poor girl." He wanted to take care of this business as quickly as possible.

Entering the Segal flat, Harry was surprised. The furniture was shabby, but everything from the sparkling china arranged on a shelf to the rag rug on the floor was clean and bright as a new pin. A box bed, where the three sisters slept, was hidden behind a curtain, white and pristine as a bride's dress. The table was set for afternoon tea with sparkling silver and dishes on a delicate lace cloth. As he was welcomed, Harry's mind was racing: "They might be poor, but this is a genteel family. Jean comes from good stock."

At first meeting, Harry was completely captivated. Jean was far prettier than her pictures. Black, curly hair framed a clear-skinned, smiling face, and a stylish silk and lace dress showed off her slim figure. Her deep brown eyes looked into his as she extended a hand in welcome.

Harry was thrilled. Not so Jean. Seeing Harry for the first time, she was shocked: "No one told me he is so old, and so much shorter than me. I hoped he would be tall." Jean was slender, statuesque—almost six feet tall in stocking feet. Harry was forty years old and five feet five inches in shoes.

Initially, as Jean made an effort to get over her shock, conversation was stilted. But because she was still sincerely interested in this man, she pressed him for information.

"Did you have a good journey? How far did you come? Tell me about Lerwick, about your shop and where you live."

Anxious to impress her, Harry described Lerwick in glowing terms. Compared to Gorodea, the *shtetl* he had left behind, Lerwick was heaven and his property palatial. He rambled on nervously. "You will like it very much. I have my own shop in my own building. Can you imagine, just a few years in Shetland and I'm able to buy a shop. And the flat above the shop is beautiful; running water, indoor toilet, and you can look out the window onto Commercial Street. My shop is right in the center—and we have so many customers."

"How do you get there?"

Avoiding an answer, he rambled on, "Oh, there is so much fish—herring, hake, halibut, whiting. I can go down to the pier and get a *fry* of herring from my friend Johnnie, the fisherman, any time. And potatoes, and carrots, and cabbage . . . all very cheap. You will be able to cook whatever you like."

Jean wasn't entirely convinced. "Come back tomorrow and I'll have an answer."

In the kitchen she sat late into the night, talking with her mother and her sisters.

Rosie and Sadie agreed. "He seems like a fine upstanding man."

Esther put her arm around Jean, "You'll be far away. But if this is what you want, you have my blessing."

"But, he's so much older than I am."

"Yes, but maybe so much wiser," quipped Sadie.

Jean wavered. "I don't know what to do. Maybe it won't be so bad. He'll be a good provider."

"You don't have much choice," Sadie scolded. "You're twenty-seven, no *nedan*, all your friends are married with half a dozen babies. Maybe you just want to be an old maid."

Jean looked at her sister with disdain. "You don't have to worry. You're leaving for Canada. I'm going to bed. I'll think about it in the morning."

She kissed her mother goodnight, and tossed and turned and agonized through the night.

Morning came too soon. Jean pulled the box-bed curtain aside. Her mother was leaning over the stove, pouring water into the teapot.

"How many more times will I see this," Jean thought. "How can I leave my mother? Sadie and Rosie will be gone and she'll be alone."

Esther straightened up, turning to look at Jean. "Have you made up your mind?"

"Yes. He seems like a good man and works hard. If I don't marry him, I may never have another chance."

Esther came over and kissed Jean on the forehead. "May God bless you and keep you, and may you always be happy."

Tearfully, Jean clung to Esther. "I don't want to leave, but what can I do?"

"You're doing the right thing. Don't worry about me. You'll make me a grandmother yet and come to me with a baby in your arms."

One week later, Jean and Harry were married in a small ceremony attended by Esther, Sadie, and Rosie. Louis Greenwald and Harry's brothers were there as well. Jean's father, Jacob, had died several months before.

"How does it feel to be Mrs. Harry Greenwald?" Sadie asked slyly.

"Don't be stupid. I don't feel any different. Well maybe just a bit excited at going to Lerwick and having my own home." Jean was practical. This was a marriage of convenience. Love was not a factor. She believed that life in Shetland would be easier than in Glasgow. But there were tears in her eyes as she kissed her mother goodbye.

Jean said little as Harry, brusque and businesslike, arranged for a first-class cabin on the steamship *St. Magnus*. He promised, "You'll

Dad, on his wedding day, 1935

have warm blankets and the steward will bring tea and biscuits before we dock." By the end of the trip, Jean couldn't look at anything resembling food. The untamed currents of the Pentland Firth make for one of the roughest crossings in the world. The ship had tossed like a cork on the Atlantic Ocean, which became more turbulent after they left the coast of the Scottish mainland. Memories of that journey were vivid years later. "I was lying in the cabin, retching and in tears. I prayed that I would die. The journey was endless and Harry was no help."

Harry loved being on the sea. He was never seasick and couldn't understand why his new wife was so ill. Nervously, he paced the corridors, muttering to anyone who would listen. "What can I do except give her sips of water which she can't keep down."

Arriving in Lerwick, Jean was so weak she could barely stand. The ground was still rolling under her feet. Clutching Harry's arm as they disembarked, she muttered, "What a way to begin a marriage."

Jean's first views of Lerwick did nothing to lift her spirits. It looked like a ghost town, where everything and everyone had gone to sleep a century ago. The town was gloomy and forbidding. Houses, in dark shadow, rose out of the water like silent sentinels. White mist swirled around the largest building, the Queens Hotel. Occasionally, the mist broke to reveal the low doors to the smugglers' *lodberries*. Victoria Pier, where the ship had docked, stretched out into the coal-black harbor like a long, sinister finger. Except for the passengers and a few dockhands, no one was about. The Town Hall clock at the top of the hill pealed out five melancholy strokes. It was five o'clock in the morning.

"There must be some mistake, Harry. You told me Lerwick is so beautiful. How could you bring me to this godforsaken place?"

In an unusual display of affection, he put his arm around his bride. "Welcome to Lerwick," his Yiddish accent thicker than she remembered it in Glasgow. After all, she had met him only a few times before the wedding.

Her mind was racing, her thoughts in turmoil. "Am I in the middle of a nightmare?"

The damp air, suffused with a sense of foreboding, penetrated her thick brown woolen coat like icy daggers. She shivered. Harry tried his best to reassure her. "It will warm up later when the fog burns off."

They walked along the pebble-strewn path leading to Commercial Street, the main thoroughfare paved with cobblestones. Jean's silver-buckled shoes, which had cost a week's wages, squelched through the mud. "They'll be ruined," she said, almost in tears. Harry glanced down, replying gruffly, "This is not the kind of shoes you wear here. We'll get you some heavy, sturdy boots."

Shrugging off his arm, Jean felt her temper beginning to rise. Angry words tumbled out. "I'm not going to wear any ugly boots. I'll find something else. There must be a shoe store in this hellish place."

Harry, anxious to change the subject, stopped in front of a little shop. In the window, shelves held jars of sweets and chocolates. The sign, Ice Cream Saloon, was painted in green and yellow above the door. "This is my shop," he said bursting with pride. "And we live upstairs."

"How do you get in? Do we go through the shop?"

Harry led her through a covered alley, the entrance to Burns Lane. He stopped in front of a brick-red door. "No one locks doors here," he said, as he lifted a tarnished brass latch and opened the door.

Harry stood aside. Jean shrank back in dismay. "Is this the storeroom? What kind of a place is this? Where's the *mezuzah* on the door?" Inside, it was dim and dank. She could just make out a winding flight of bare wooden stairs. "This is where I'm supposed to live?"

"It's fine once you get upstairs," he answered, taking her by the arm and pushing her up the stairway.

"I can't believe this," she stammered. "You really expect me to stay here?"

He didn't answer. They entered the most depressing room she had ever seen.

"I left Glasgow for this?" she thought. A bare electric lightbulb hung from the ceiling—next to it, sticky flypaper, black with dead flies. Two small-paned windows overlooking the street were caked with salt and grime; faded, cracked linoleum covered the creaky floor, and the fireplace was so choked with ashes that the fire barely glowed. The dried-up remains of a past meal encrusted chipped plates, piled up on a bare wooden table.

She was appalled. Thoughts were buzzing inside her head. "I must leave. I can't stay." Aloud she said, "Where's the sink?"

Harry led Jean into the narrow hallway, where cold water trickled out of a grimy brass faucet into the brown-stained porcelain sink. "You have to fill a kettle of water, heat it on the stove so that there's hot water to wash dishes."

Worse was to come. "And where's the toilet?" Down two steps, a narrow door led into a little room with a toilet. A chain hung down from the overhead cistern. "Pull to flush," said Harry. Neat squares of *The Shetland Times* hung from a nearby nail. A tiny, grimy window opened out onto the lane.

"Who knew from soft, white toilet paper," chuckled Ma, when she described this to us decades later.

Before she could speak, Harry pointed to a zinc bathtub hanging on the back of the door. "If you want to take a bath, you can heat kettles of water and then pour it into this tub. You'll be warm if you set the tub in front of the fire." He added, " you have to keep a good fire going."

"And how am I to do that? Who's going to drag buckets of coal up here?"

Harry assured her. "I'll do that. I always keep the fire going."

Jean's tone sharpened. She was becoming more angry than shocked. "Glad to hear that. I'll have enough to do."

There were two more rooms on the same floor as the kitchen. "Are these the bedrooms?"

"No, no. I keep stock and old furniture in there. The bedroom is on the next floor up."

Jean was dazed. An enormous room, which was the bedroom, was as bad, if not worse than, the kitchen. The sheets were clean, but the blankets were tangled and both big beds were unmade. The wooden floor was bare—not even a rug at the side of the bed—and the only heat would come from an ash-covered potbellied stove in the corner.

Jean's shock turned to fury. "I'm leaving. You don't need a wife— you need a team of scavengers."

Harry, beginning to get worried, tried to reassure her. Then he added, "You can't leave now; the boat has left and doesn't come back until next week. That is, if the weather holds. It's a mess, but you'll get it cleaned up."

"Not without help," she shot back.

"I'll get some women in tomorrow." he promised.

Rushing downstairs and out into the street, he gave a passing young boy a shilling and a note. "Take this to Cathy Laurenson on Hill Street and be quick." Cathy occasionally helped in the shop. "I need you to come and help my wife clean the house," the note read. "It's only for a day."

Cathy stayed for two weeks. She was completely bewildered. "I never knew he lived in this mess. When he stays with us in the country, he's so clean and organized. He's constantly washing his hands after he pets the dogs. Newspapers are always neatly folded, and he makes up his bed before he leaves. My mother always says that you'd never know he's been in the house."

"Well, now you know," Jean replied grimly.

All the while she was cleaning and cooking, Jean struggled for a way to get out of what she thought of as "this catastrophe." Jean and Harry were two opposites, each without understanding or patience for the other. She was articulate, bright, and slow to lose her temper; he was moody and critical, with a volatile temper.

What to do? Divorce was a *shandig*. How could she admit to her family that she couldn't stay married and live "in the backwoods." She had quit her job. She couldn't go back to Glasgow. "We were like oil and water," she would later say sadly. "I knew I had to sink or swim, and I decided to swim. How could I do otherwise?" she told me. "At least I had my own house. Then you children came, so I worked to make it livable." She added, "I could never have left my children."

Cathy and Jean worked to make the rooms not just livable, but comfortable and clean. At the end of two weeks, they had washed the windows until they sparkled, polished the black and chrome stove to a high gloss, and covered the bare electric lightbulb with a cut-glass lamp shade, so that the kitchen was bathed in soft, amber light. Jean bullied Harry into taking the battered kitchen furniture to the dump and burning it.

Each week on a Wednesday afternoon, when the shops were closed, a furniture auction was held in a cavernous old warehouse. Jean had a good eye for quality, albeit second- or third-hand. Although she was a stranger, one of her first forays into Lerwick "society" was to "the sale room." Now that most of the furniture had been taken to the dump, the rooms were bare. "I can't live without some good furniture," Jean insisted, ignoring Harry's reluctance. Besides, with a variety of furniture and bric-a-brac being sold, the auction was a social event. Women brought folding chairs or sat on long wooden benches, busily knitting the Fair Isle scarves and gloves they would sell to English department stores. Hot, sweet tea from thermos flasks was passed around and there were always chocolate biscuits to go along. Jean made friends. At first, the Lerwick women felt sorry for the young "foreign" woman; anyone not born and bred in Shetland was foreign. But sympathy grew into respect as they enjoyed her company and caught on to her Glasgow accent.

Jean was an aggressive but shrewd bidder. She acquired a mahogany drop-leaf table (now in my American living room) and matching chairs with red leather seats. She had no trouble justifying her purchases. "We can't sit on these *shoogly* chairs, and that table was a disgrace."

Bright new linoleum was laid on the floor, and Jean, an accomplished seamstress, hurried to sew white, lacy curtains on her Singer sewing machine, one of the few items she had brought from Glasgow. "I won't have these people staring into my kitchen." The offices of The Cooperative, a grocery store, were directly across from the kitchen windows. A bright white oilcloth, with a pattern of yellow and red flowers covered the new table "so that it won't be marked up with tea stains and hot plates." In the bedroom were two double beds, "one for visitors." Each was made up with new linens from the shop's stockroom, and colorful patchwork rugs, made from pieces of felt and tweed, covered the newly scrubbed floor. Even the potbellied stove was burnished to a dull sheen.

The chimney sweep was called in, but only after the chimney had caught fire, and smoke and flames were belching high into the sky. Jean was positive "it had not been swept for years." The fire truck arrived, sirens wailing, and while neighbors gathered to watch, the flames were extinguished. The fire in the Greenwalds' *lum* was the topic of conversation for the next week.

In response to a frantic letter from Jean, Sadie and Rosie had sent a *mezuzah*.

"Now I feel that this is a home," sighed Jean as Harry hammered in the last brad attaching it to the Burns Lane doorpost.

Harry was delighted with the transformation. "You've spent a lot of money but my, my, you've done a good job." One of his rare compliments.

Jean just shrugged. "I hope you appreciate it."

Hard work and a dour husband were beginning to take their toll. She became adept at doling out threats. "If you don't keep the fire stoked up, I can't cook." The coal shed was downstairs in the lane, but Harry made sure that there was always a full bucket of coal at the side of the stove. Jean was a superb cook, preparing all the Ashkenazi dishes that he loved: fresh beet borscht, potato *kugels,* and raisin–coconut strudels. He had no desire to jeopardize his good fortune. For the first time in his life, he was eating bounteously and well.

"BUTTER"-CRUSTED
VEGETABLE KUGEL

SERVES 6 TO 8

Root vegetables such as potatoes, turnips, and carrots were stored over the winter. Lacking matzo meal, Ma used brown breadcrumbs to bind the mixture and grated the vegetables on a hand-held grater. Today, a food processor makes preparation quick and easy.

2 medium leeks, split and trimmed
6 tablespoons olive oil, divided
2 large baking potatoes, peeled
1 large yellow turnip, peeled
2 large carrots, peeled
2 cloves garlic, minced
3 eggs, lightly beaten
2 cups soft brown breadcrumbs, divided
$\frac{1}{4}$ cup chopped fresh parsley, packed, or 2 tablespoons dried
salt and white pepper to taste
2 tablespoons margarine

Preheat oven to 350°F. Spray a 9-inch-square baking dish with nonstick cooking spray or brush generously with olive oil. Set aside.

Slice leeks thinly. Wash well in cold water. Drain. Heat 2 tablespoons olive oil in a large pot over medium heat. Add the sliced leek. Reduce heat to low and sauté for 10 minutes.

While the leek is cooking, cut the potatoes, turnip, and carrots in chunks. Grate in the food processor, using the grater blade. Add to the leeks along with the garlic. Sauté for 10 minutes longer, or until vegetables have lost their raw look. Transfer to a bowl. Stir in the remaining oil, eggs, 1 cup breadcrumbs, and parsley. Season with salt and white pepper to taste.

Spoon into prepared baking dish. Melt margarine in a small skillet over high heat. Add the remaining breadcrumbs and stir quickly until margarine is absorbed. Sprinkle over the *kugel* in baking dish. Bake in preheated oven for 1 hour or until nicely browned and cooked in center. Test with a knife. Vegetables should be soft, underneath a crisp crust.

PEG'S BOILED
FRUIT LOAF

MAKES 1 LOAF
(9 X 5 X 3-INCH)

Ma's friend Peg was a splendid baker. When we visited, slices of buttered fruit loaf were served on a plate along with hot, sweet tea poured into fine china cups. This is a good, moist fruit loaf, which keeps, tightly wrapped, at cool room temperature for up to a week. Good either sliced and spread with butter or toasted.

2 cups mixed dried fruit, chopped

1 cup sugar

1 cup water

½ stick (4 tablespoons) margarine

1 teaspoon baking soda

1 large egg, lightly beaten

pinch salt

2 cups self-rising flour

Preheat oven to 350°F. Grease a 9 x 5 x 3-inch loaf pan.

Place dried fruit, sugar, water, margarine, and baking soda in a saucepan. Bring to a boil over medium-high heat. Lower heat to simmer and continue cooking for 5 minutes. Cool to room temperature. Beat in the egg and salt. Gradually add the self-rising flour, beating well.

Pour into prepared loaf pan. Bake ¾ to 1 hour in preheated oven or until a toothpick inserted in center comes out clean (Ma used a steel-bladed knife). Cool on a wire rack.

MA'S "ROLY-POLY"

We called Ma's strudel a "roly-poly." Crisp short-crust pastry was filled with handfuls of whatever dried fruits were available, but dried coconut and homemade blackcurrant jam were always included.

PASTRY
2 cups all-purpose flour
pinch salt
6 tablespoons margarine
2–3 tablespoons cold water to mix

FILLING
2 tablespoons blackcurrant jam
$\frac{1}{2}$ cup raisins
$\frac{1}{4}$ cup currants
$\frac{1}{4}$ cup diced, crystallized orange peel
2 tablespoons shredded, unsweetened coconut
cinnamon and sugar to sprinkle

Preheat oven to 375°F. Grease a baking sheet or spray with nonstick cooking spray.

In a bowl, mix the flour and salt. Rub or cut in the margarine until mixture is the consistency of fine breadcrumbs. Add enough cold water to form a stiff dough. This may be done in the food processor. Add enough water for mixture to form a ball.

Turn dough out onto a floured board. Roll into a rectangle, about 10 x 8 inches. Spread jam on dough to within $\frac{1}{4}$ inch of edges. Sprinkle raisins, currants, and orange peel over jam. Top with a sprinkling of coconut and dust lightly with cinnamon. Roll up like a jellyroll, pressing edges to seal. Place seam-side down on prepared baking sheet. Prick surface all over with a fork. Brush with water and sprinkle with sugar. Bake in preheated oven for 30 minutes or until pastry is golden brown. Cool before slicing with a serrated knife.

4

A New Beginning

One of the few joys of Jean's first days in Lerwick was breakfast with a soft, floury roll, warm from the ovens of Malcolmson's bakery three doors down the street. July was unusually warm, and yeasty aromas floated in the air. Jean knew she was pregnant when she was so sick she could barely crawl out of bed. In the first months of her pregnancy, the smells were nauseating.

"I can't move the bakery," said Harry in a sympathetic moment. "Maybe you want to go live in the country for a while?" He knew many of the *crofters* would be happy to have her stay for a few shillings a week.

"To be with strangers? Never!"

Jean struggled through the next six months. "How am I going to get through this?"

She had no friends to confide in, and Harry was gone much of the time, selling jewelry in the country. He was caring, but not capable of giving Jean the pampering she so sorely needed. Of the two doctors, one was a habitual drunk, the other a womanizer. Women delivered at home with a midwife. If there were complications, there was little the cottage hospital could do. Jean was adamant. "I'll go to Glasgow a month before my due date. At least I'll have a competent doctor there."

Then word came that her mother had died. Jean was devastated. "I have to leave at once."

According to Jewish law, a funeral must take place within twenty-four hours, but it was three more days before she could get a boat to Aberdeen and from there a train to Glasgow. Sadie and Rose were on the station platform to meet her.

Jean burst into tears. "I didn't get to say goodbye," she cried. "She won't ever be able to see my baby."

Her sisters tried to comfort her. Rosie handed her a handkerchief. "Dry your tears, don't cry. Now she is at peace, and she will look down on your baby and be proud."

But Jean couldn't stop sobbing. Sadie was concerned. Though the youngest of the three sisters, Jean had always been the strong one. "Why are you crying so much? Something else is wrong. Tell us."

"Lerwick is an uncivilized place and Harry is a cold man. Sometimes he doesn't even talk to me." She went on. "We're the only Jews there, and there's not even a kosher butcher. I'm not going back."

Sadie was frantic. She and Rosie were leaving Glasgow soon after the baby's birth. "But with a little baby what can you do here? We're leaving, you'll have no place to stay, and, if you could find a job, who will take care of the baby?"

Jean stayed with her sisters until she gave birth. Harry had arranged for her to deliver at St. Mary's Hospital, one of the best private hospitals in the city. "Your sisters will be with you, so I don't need to come," he told her.

I was born on April 24, a year after my mother had arrived in Shetland. In memory of my grandmother, I was named Esther in Hebrew, and Ethel in English. We sailed back on the *St. Magnus* at the end of May. My mother was surprised to feel relieved. She admitted, "I was sick and tired of being cooped up in that tenement. I missed the fresh air, and I liked being mistress of my own house."

Ma, holding baby Ethel

Harry paced impatiently along the pier. Usually unemotional, he was now excited. He couldn't wait to see his baby daughter. By now, I was six weeks old. Jean came down the gangplank, gently cradling me on a big white pillow. Harry looked down into big brown eyes, the beginning of a lifelong infatuation. From that moment, I could do no wrong. "I think she looks like me," he said.

Jean ignored him, instead answering, "She's so calm and sweet-tempered. The boat rolled and tossed, but there was never a whimper unless she was hungry, and I took care of that." Fortunately, on this trip, Jean was not seasick, telling her husband, "Maybe because I had to take care of Ethel and didn't have time to think about it." In fact, she had enjoyed the attention. On the voyage to Shetland, an attentive stewardess, who frequently popped into the cabin to admire the new baby, had served tea and biscuits.

Harry was an overprotective father. For the most part, I smiled, gurgled, and was content. But the moment I cried, he rushed upstairs from the shop, yelling at my mother, "What did you do? Why is she crying?" Jean was always to blame. Crying aggravated and upset Harry. His perception of children was that they should be quiet, obedient little people, seen but not heard. Jean's attitude on child rearing was completely different. "Let them run, play, and scream if they want. They're only young once." So Harry took off for the country, selling jewelry wherever he could. Jean was left to take charge of the shop, the house, and a new baby.

The new baby brought a change that made life bearable and even happier for Jean. I became the focus of attention. When she pushed the high, navy-blue baby carriage along the street, men and women would stop to admire. "What's her name? How old is she? It's the custom here to cross her hand with silver," they said, as they pressed a silver shilling or half a crown into my little fist. Jean was beginning to get acquainted with some of the women. Not only had she become very comfortable with the Shetland dialect, but also the locals were now at home with her Glasgow brogue, a recognizable Scottish lilt she kept to the end of her days. She was adamant. "I have to keep my identity. Why would I want to talk like everybody else?"

No one had a refrigerator, so the women shopped daily in the little storefront, family-owned stores along each side of Commercial Street. Jean's favorite stop was the fish market, two outdoor stalls at the edge of the pier, where it was convenient for the fishing boats to unload the day's catch. Jean was selective. She would buy only the freshest fish, those that were still squirming in the wooden boxes. Bessie—we never knew her last name—owned one stall, and Mrs. Jamison, the other. Both women were on the pier at dawn to bargain for the day's catch. They were dressed in knee-high rubber boots ("so we don't slip from the stall into the sea," joked Bessie), fingerless woolen gloves, and thick, warm shawls wrapped around head and shoulders.

There the similarity ended. Bessie was spare and wiry, with salt-crusted spectacles balanced on the end of her nose. Mrs. Jamison was buxom. Besides the *moorit* shawl she wore, she topped off her costume with a battered, brown velour hat, sporting an ostrich feather and jammed on top of her head.

The two women were fiercely competitive. "Fresh hake. You won't get it cheaper!" yelled Bessie. In response, Mrs. Jamison roared, "Come here for the best hake. It's cheap, fresh, and I'll throw in the roe." Not only did she throw in the roe or livers, but, in a flash, she also slammed the fish down on the slate slab, thereupon abruptly ending its squirming. She gutted the fish—one slit down the belly with a sharp knife—then wrapped it in old copies of *The Shetland Times*.

Harry favored Bessie. "She lives just up the lane and comes in for a bar of chocolate now and again." But for Jean, Mrs. Jamison won out. "She's clean. The floors, counters, scales—everything in the stall is hosed down at the end of the day. Bessie's filleting slab is thick with dried-up fish scales, never washed down from one day to the next." Harry was obsessive about cleanliness, so that was the end of the discussion.

Jean didn't add that she already had an ally in Mrs. Jamison, who ran the stall single-handedly, while her husband only occasionally put in an appearance. Mrs. Jamison felt sorry for the lonely young woman and always made Jean feel special. "Here's a nice piece of halibut. I've been keeping it just for you. You just cook it up in a pan of boiling water and salt. It's sweeter than hake." She weighed the fish on a scale hanging in the back of the stall. Jean paid, saying diplomatically, "I wouldn't boil it. It's better in a sweet and sour sauce."

Mrs. Jamison was curious. "How do you do that? Maybe when I have time you'll show me."

She never had the time, but in return for fish Jean brought her a dish of sweet and sour halibut. Mrs. Jamison was delighted. "Isn't that chust beautiful." And Jean's fame as an exotic cook spread up and down the lanes.

In Shetland, winter temperatures rarely go below forty degrees—
"mild for the time of year," according to the locals. Harry insisted, "only
the best for Ethel." The navy-blue carriage, made by Pedigree, a manufacturer of luxury baby carriages, was shipped from Aberdeen, attract-
ing a lot of attention. Jean grumbled, "A waste of money. An ordinary
carriage would be just fine." But unless there were gale force winds,
she wrapped me snugly in a Shetland shawl, propped me in the baby
carriage, and pushed it up the steep lane to Gilbertson Park. "The
bairn needs fresh air," she declared. That was another bone of con-
tention between my parents. Jean kept the windows open summer and
winter. Harry went behind her and closed them.

For Harry, it was convenient to live above the shop. For Jean, his
constant trips upstairs from the shop made her life miserable. Harry
had become increasingly difficult. He blamed Jean for whatever went
wrong, whether the baby was making too much noise or supplies were
late coming from Glasgow. They shouted and yelled. Then came days
of silence, when they barely exchanged words.

Jean tried to explain. "It's only natural for a baby to cry, and if
she falls she'll pick herself up." Her words fell on deaf ears, and Harry
would put on a pleasant face, retreating to face his customers.

The park was a gathering place for mothers and children, old-
age pensioners out for a stroll, and people taking a shortcut from
Burgh Road to Gilbertson Road. On her first visit, Jean made a lifelong
friend. She was resting on a wooden bench when a tall, well-dressed
woman walked over. "My, my, what a *bonnie, peerie* lass," she said,
peering into the carriage. The *peerie* lass was now three months old,
and Lillie Hunter, who had been head cook to a wealthy English family,
had returned home to get married. They exchanged introductions. "I
know who you are," said Lillie with a warm smile. "You're Harry
Greenwald's wife. The whole of Shetland knows you're here."

"How can that be," stammered Jean. "I'm not that long in Lerwick."

Lillie was reassuring. "This is a small town. We all know each
other here, and you'll fit in just fine." From that moment, Lillie and her
husband adopted the insecure young woman. Lillie became Granny
Hunter to the Greenwald family. Twenty years older, she became
Jean's trusted confidante. When Lillie died, Jean mourned, "I've lost
my dearest friend."

Harry made breakfast each morning, porridge made the true
Scots way. Oatmeal, a pinch of salt, and water, all stirred together with
a *spurtle*, a long, slender wooden stick that could get into the corners

Granny Hunter, in village of Billister,
drystone wall (no cement used) in
background

of the pan, keeping the porridge from getting lumpy. Then he would
change his beret for a peaked cap and go downstairs to the shop.

He had a strict routine. Jean had dinner ready on the table at
one o'clock. Then he stretched out on an armchair for a fifteen-minute
nap. Refreshed, he ran downstairs to open the shop for afternoon
business. After supper, Harry set up a green felt-covered card table in
a corner and worked on the bills. His bookkeeping was meticulous.
They exchanged few words.

Jean once wrote to her sister, Sadie, "I'm sure Harry doesn't love
me. I'm just a housekeeper here to cater to his every need. I have no
one to talk to."

It seemed to Jean that all her friends and neighbors had good
marriages. They didn't argue or shout at each other, at least not in
public. In those days, the least hint of family discord was hushed up. It
was something to be ashamed of, and on no account should any argu-
ments be made public. Jean was saddened."Harry and me, we're just
like oil and water; we can't agree on anything."

Jean gained weight after my birth, giving Harry another reason
to humiliate her at every turn. The undeserved criticism and blame
left her in tears. On these frequent occasions, she dressed me in a
warm coat and leggings, and we went downstairs into the street.
"Today, all he'll get is *mince and tatties*," she would say on our way to
the butcher. Good-natured banter from the butcher and a cup of tea in
the café restored some degree of normalcy and calm, so that she could

return home and ignore her husband. Ironically, Harry's customers regarded him as "a real fine fellow, even though he's a *Sooth-moother*."

As a young mother, with no family nearby, Jean yearned for a kind word or gentle touch, or, at the very least, another woman she could talk to. If Harry had been supportive and caring, Jean's life would have been tolerable. But though she was articulate, bright, and outgoing, Harry was moody, prone to outbursts of temper, and always critical.

Finally, when she could bear it no longer, she packed a suitcase and ran to Granny Hunter, with me in her arms.

"I must get away from here," she cried. "I can't live like this. He's so lovely to other folk but to me he's cold and angry."

Yet she knew she couldn't leave and take me with her. "How will we both survive?" Then sadly, she said, "I'm trapped." So she pulled herself together, looked at me, and said, "We'll have to make the best of it. You and me."

Granny Hunter soothed and comforted. "Sit down here by the fire and tell me about it." After numerous cups of hot sweet tea and thick slices of *brunnie,* slathered with fresh-churned butter, Jean calmed down.

"You know you can always come to me. I'll never say a word to a soul," Lillie said kindly.

Jean dried her tears and splashed her face with cold water. Mother and child walked slowly back to Burns Lane. Late that night, when Harry was checking inventory in the stockroom, she unpacked the suitcase.

GRANNY'S
BUTTERMILK BRUNNIE

Granny Hunter adapted some of the ingredients and cooking methods learned in England to Shetland cooking. In her version of a Shetland scone, fennel-scented, crusty wedges are brushed with a sugary glaze. Best eaten warm from the oven, with sweet butter. Wrap leftovers in a clean tea towel and toast for breakfast.

PASTRY
2 cups self-rising flour
$1/4$ cup steel-cut oatmeal
$1/2$ teaspoon salt
$1/4$ cup dark brown sugar, lightly packed
2 teaspoons ground allspice
2 teaspoons fennel seeds
1 cup raisins
1 egg
3 tablespoons molasses
$3/4$ cup buttermilk

SUGAR GLAZE
$1/4$ cup sugar
3 tablespoons confectioners sugar
2 tablespoons water

Preheat oven to 350°F. Spray a 10-inch pie pan with nonstick cooking spray.

Place the flour, oatmeal, salt, sugar, allspice, fennel seeds, and raisins in a bowl. Stir to mix. Make a well in center. Stir in the egg, molasses, and buttermilk. Dough should be slightly sticky.

Turn out onto a floured board. Pat into a round, about $3/4$-inch thick. Cut into 8 wedges. Place on prepared pan. Bake in preheated oven for 30 minutes, or until a toothpick inserted comes out clean. While wedges are still warm, prick the tops all over with a fork. Pour sugar glaze over, spreading with a spoon or brush.

Sugar Glaze: In a small bowl, stir all glaze ingredients together. Microwave on High for 1 minute. Stir to dissolve sugar. Microwave on Medium 1 minute longer. Spread glaze as directed above.

SWEET AND
SOUR HALIBUT

SERVES 4

Ma didn't have time for "fussy cooking." This recipe illustrates her talent for enhancing fish fresh from the sea with a simple Béchamel sauce.

1 small onion, sliced
2 bay leaves
2 tablespoons sugar, or to taste
$\frac{1}{3}$ cup cider vinegar
4 halibut steaks, about 6 ounces each
salt and white pepper
2 eggs
lemon wedges and parsley to garnish (optional)

Pour about $1\frac{1}{2}$ cups boiling water into a shallow saucepan. Add the onion and bay leaves. Cover partially and bring to simmer over medium heat. Cook for 5 minutes. Stir in the sugar and vinegar. Add halibut, arranging in one layer. Sprinkle with salt and pepper. Cover and simmer for 20 minutes, or until fish flakes are opaque when separated with tines of a fork.

Using a slotted spoon, transfer fish to a platter. Set aside. Strain the fish stock. Cool and whisk into the eggs. Return mixture to the saucepan, and whisk continuously over medium heat until thickened. Do not boil. Adjust seasoning. Pour sauce over the fish. Garnish with lemon wedges and parsley (optional).

Neighbors often stopped by with half a dozen brown trout caught in country lochs. Jean transformed leftover cooked trout into this hearty pie served at teatime, the evening meal. Cooked salmon may be substituted for trout.

1 tablespoon butter or margarine
1 small onion, diced
3 cups cooked trout, flaked
2 tablespoons mayonnaise
2 tablespoons light cream
1 cup canned or frozen thawed peas
salt and white pepper
4 cups mashed potatoes
$\frac{1}{2}$ cup grated sharp cheese (cheddar)
paprika and dried dill to garnish

Preheat oven to 375°F. Heat butter or margarine in a medium pan over medium heat. Add the onion and cook until softened, about 5 minutes. Add the trout, mayonnaise, cream, peas, and salt and pepper to taste. Mix well.

Transfer to a $1\frac{1}{2}$-quart ovenproof dish. Cover with mashed potatoes and scatter cheese over the top. Sprinkle with paprika and dried dill. Bake in preheated oven for 30 minutes, or until top is golden. Serve hot.

5

"You Can Get It at Greenvald's"

In the early twentieth century, Jewish-owned stores in the American South were called "Jew stores." Not so in Shetland. It was never the Jew store. From the first day the Greenwalds set up shop, locals would say "you can get it at Greenvald's." It became the slogan for a tiny storefront, where everything from candy to condoms were sold. Though Grandfather Louis Greenwald recorded the name with a *w* in the Shetland Archives, Shetlanders pronounced the *w* as a *v*, perhaps reverting to the Old Norse alphabet. The name continued until the stores were sold in 1991.

Greenwald's was in a prime location: smack in the middle of Commercial Street and facing a pathway down to the pier, so the townsfolk had to pass no matter where they were going. The opposite building housed The Cooperative, a pre–World War II version of the supermarket. Islanders bought at least a few staples there in order to cash in on dividend coupons they could redeem for a saucepan or a clock. A gilded clock, bought with coupons from the "Co-op," was the focal point on many a fireplace mantel. The pink granite building on the corner, where Dad did all his banking business, is still the Clydesdale Bank.

Two rival bakeries, Malcolmson's and Blance's, three *sweetie* shops, a shoe store, and several everyday clothing stores were all just steps away. Shop doors opened promptly at 9 A.M., and the street, which had been deserted except for a few fishermen strolling down to their boats, burst into lively activity. Window shades were rolled up to reveal merchandise displays. Hunks of beef and unplucked chickens hung in the butcher shops, and lamb chops and tripe were arranged on white enamel trays. There were bottles of wine, jars of jam, and condiments such as HP Sauce in the grocer's, where pimply-faced young shop assistants, with blue denim aprons tied around their waists, dusted jars and bottles with feather dusters in preparation for a new day. Necessities such as bottles of aspirin, saccharin, bandages, and stone hot-water bottles (placed between the sheets to warm the beds) filled the window of the Medical Hall, the chemist's shop.

My favorite shop was Pottinger's Grocer and Fine Comestibles. Entering, I was whisked into a dimly lit, aromatic "Aladdin's" cave. There stood wooden barrels of glistening, grainy demerera sugar, each with a silver scoop hanging on a chain over the side, ready for measuring into brown paper bags. Slabs of golden butter, cut into half-pound pieces and wrapped in wax paper, rested on chilled marble. Wheels of cheese gave off a mouthwatering pungency, and exotic spices filled the store with a magical perfume when their tight-lidded tins were opened. Dusty bottles of wine and a constant supply of the best malt whisky were stacked on high shelves. At the end of winter, when we had run out of Ma's preserves, we might include jam on our shopping list. For housewives, no trip to "the street" was complete without stopping for a cup of tea and a bit of gossip in one of the many tearooms.

Ice cream was a luxury never tasted or dreamed of in the Gorodea *shtetl*, so perhaps it was only natural that the first Greenwald shop started out as an Ice Cream Saloon. I vividly remember the white wrought-iron table with two wooden folding chairs set up in front of the counter, leaving just enough room for customers to buy their daily chocolate fix. Shetlanders, like all Scots, adore sweet things. Arranged on shelves behind the counter, tall glass jars were kept filled with a colorful variety of *sweeties*: there were striped hard candies, red aniseed balls, liquorice allsorts, and *pandrops*. Business was constant, if not brisk, and a steady stream of customers squeezed through the double, glass-paneled door. Although there were three other sweet shops on the street, many folks preferred Greenvald's. Along with their purchases, they could be sure of a joke with international flavor. Dad was a completely different personality in the shop. He was outgoing and liked nothing better than long discussions with customers, who soon became friends. With an impish grin lighting his face and a subtlety envied by fellow shopkeepers, he sold the locals more than they came in for, and they cheerfully paid up. The townsfolk loved Harry.

Dad couldn't afford an ice cream machine, so he approached Mr. Curatolli, an Italian who had introduced the sweet, frozen confection to Lerwegians.

"I would like to buy ice cream for my saloon. I don't need much, maybe a gallon."

Mr. Curatolli was a jovial man, who, like my father, still had an accent."Come along at nine o'clock tomorrow morning. Maybe we can do business."

They came to an agreement. Dad got the ice cream he needed. In return, each week Mr. Curatolli picked out a brooch or silver bauble from the blue velvet tray in the leather case.

Getting the frozen confection to the shop was a major production. First thing in the morning, Dad took his wheelbarrow to the icehouse, a windowless building with thick stone walls, on the shady side of the street. A block of dry ice was loaded onto the barrow. Back at the ice cream saloon, he searched under the counter. "Where's the ice pick?"

"Same place you put it yesterday!" Ma yelled back. Finally, casting aside boxes and tools, he dragged out a rusty ice pick. "Found it. You must have hidden it."

After the arduous process of chipping away a cavity big enough for a milk pail, Dad threw a clean white cloth over the ice. Only then did he saunter, swinging pail in hand, along Commercial Street to Curatolli's shop. There were stops along the way for a *yarn* and invitations to stop by one of the boats for a *fry* of fat mackerel. But on the way back he was an Olympic sprinter, rushing to set the ice cream in the ice before it started to melt.

Each day before breakfast, Ma baked a batch of *kichel*—light, sugar-crusted cookies, whose delicate aromas drifted downstairs to the shop. One cookie was tucked into the corner of each dish of ice cream. Customers raved about her baked goods, especially if Dad was within earshot. They teased him. "Jean, the *biscuits* are far better than the ice cream."

Dad was the consummate shopkeeper. On a busy day, customers crowded into the long space in front of the counter, where—under glass—watches, rings, necklaces, and brooches were displayed. The Burra Isle fisherman may have come in for cigarettes, but he came away with "a little bauble" for the wife or sweetheart.

Handing the packet of Players over the counter, Dad casually pointed to a gold brooch set with semiprecious rubies. "This just came in from Glasgow. *Bonnie*, isn't it?"

"Let me have a look. . . ."

Dad removed the brooch from its royal-blue velvet case, carefully holding the edges with two fingers, so as not to dull the shiny gold frame.

"Wouldn't this be a fine surprise for Jennie. See the workmanship—beautiful isn't it?"

"And how much would this be?"

Dad laughed, "Come on. You can afford it. This was a good week for the fishing. You got top prices."

"Harry, give me a good price and maybe I will. Jennie's working hard taking care of the *bairns* and the outside work, and me away so much."

Dad paused to give thought—his cost plus a reasonable profit.

"Three pounds ten shillings," Dad said, adding, "and I'm giving it to you at cost, no profit to me."

"Fine. Wrap it up."

With conversation and banter, Dad had broken down any final resistance. Dad and the Burra fisherman were delighted. Dad had made a sale, but, almost as important, both men had thoroughly enjoyed the bargaining. The fisherman felt he got rock-bottom price, Dad made a profit, and Jennie was thrilled with an unexpected gift. Locals would say good-naturedly, "Harry can sell you the shirt off your back." Greenwald's quickly built up a reputation for fair prices, good quality, and the bonus—great entertainment in the process.

The slogan, "You can always get it at Greenvald's," was coined by the whole community. People often phoned orders. "I need two pairs of trousers, size 46. A *bonnie peenie* for Maggie, extra large, and a pound of *pandrops*—I've been having some indigestion lately— and a packet of Mitchell's Triple X chewing tobacco." Dad would get it all together, parcel it up with heavy brown paper and thick string, and deliver it to the next outgoing bus or ferry.

It was the habit of fishermen and *crofters* to chew tobacco for a bit, then spit into a glowing peat fire, or if they were in the shop, open the door and spit out into the street, mercifully avoiding passersby. In Greenwald's shop, a sign, half-hidden behind boxes on the counter warned, "No spitting allowed in here."

The only heating in the shop came from a cast-iron stove. As more stock was added, a paraffin heater that stood in a corner replaced the stove.The stove now served as an extra shelf on which boxes of woolen socks and lisle and silk stockings were heaped high. Although electricity had been connected to all the Commercial Street shops, Dad felt there still wasn't enough light to view his stock. Several Tilley lamps in brass holders were hung in dark corners. Paraffin filled the bottom bowls, and tall, slim vaporizers led to delicate mantles protected by shades of milky white glass. Frequently—every hour or so—Dad had to pump up the lamps to keep them bright.

Much of the business came from *crofters* and fishermen, clad in the traditional garb that identified their trades. The women were warmly wrapped in shawls knitted in the natural wool colors of fawn and dark brown—for "a day in the town." By contrast, Dad was spiffy in a brown-and-white-striped starched shirt, its collar fastened with a silver stud, a conservative tie, and shoes so highly polished they shone like glass. Ma spent precious hours ironing, until finally she gave up. "You can iron your own damn shirts. I have the house, shop, and the *bairns* to look after."

Once again, help came from Cathy. "Oh, Mrs. Greenwald, I'd love to come in and do the ironing. The work on this *croft* is killing me."

Fortunately, ice cream and *sweeties* were not our only source of income. Dad left for days at a time, traveling to the *crofts*. To get to the outlying islands of Fetlar and Yell, he boarded a little ferryboat, his bicycle and packages hoisted along with him.

For the most part, each *croft* was self-supporting, with a cow for milk—some of which was churned into butter and cheese, the residue into a cooling buttermilk—and plenty of fish for the taking in the crystal-clear waters of the *voe*. Every household grew enough potatoes, cabbage, and root vegetables, and stored them in an outdoor shed. With a barrel of salt herring, and rhubarb transformed into jars of ruby-red jam, a *crofter* had plenty of food to last over the winter.

Dad, with his supply of clothing, jewelry, and spectacles, was always warmly welcomed. Children's clothes were made at home from homespun tweed and hand-knitted sweaters. My brother Roy recalls that "for women, their wrap-around *peenies* with a bright floral pattern on a black background—for those in mourning, the floral patterns were lilac—these were best-sellers. Boxes of thick brown lisle stockings in all sizes were stacked above the stove. Flannel nightgowns, fleecy, lined knickers with matching petticoats in pink, blue, and beige were in great demand in the winter months of September through March." Greenwald's also carried a few corsets, but Roy chuckled that "Dad didn't carry many, as there were no trying-on facilities."

For the men, Dad brought triple-thick-ribbed long underwear, essential while working on the boats at sea. According to his practiced sales pitch, "the finest is pure wool." Burra fishermen wore only trousers of heavy navy serge, material that was warm and hard-wearing. Ma's comment when she saw them piled up in the shop, along with black heavy-duty suspenders: "They wear like iron. They'll never wear out and that's bad for business."

Dad was also the traveling "optician," offering a service lacking to the country folk. By today's standards, his testing methods were unorthodox to say the least. Picking up a copy of *The Shetland Times* or maybe *The Shetland News* (there were two newspapers in the early half of the twentieth century), he asked, in his heavy Yiddish accent, "Can you read this clearly?"

"Well, it's a *peerie* bit blurry."

He opened a leather case containing a selection of wire-framed spectacles, with a white, numbered label attached to each pair. Roy remembers it was customary to start with a number 6, the weakest lens strength, and work upwards until they could read the small print. The cost: 1/6 pence a pair. "And you get the case for free." People were incredibly grateful. They might not have been able to read or see clearly for years. After the transactions were completed, tea was poured into the best china cups and served with *bannocks* smeared with fresh butter. And Dad always had a good *yarn* for the crofters, who were hungry for news from neighboring villages. These country roads had no streetlights. So, when darkness fell, Dad was invited to sleep over.

In 1937, the ice cream table and chairs were abandoned to make room for everyday work-wear for men and women. A long wooden plank on three-inch blocks was laid on the floor behind the counter so that Dad's five-foot, five-inch frame could be raised to see eye to eye with customers. The ice cream saloon was now a clothing store. Ma had learned to choose her battles, and the renovated store was one of them. "This shop must be in my name, too." A freshly painted, green and gold sign above the shop now read, "H & J Greenwald, Fine Drapers."

Dad ordered so much stock that the wooden shelves were crammed from floor to ceiling with bundles of towels and sheets, men's underwear, and women's overalls, all tied with thick string just as they had been pulled from the mailed packages. A Frys chocolate display cabinet at one end of the counter was no longer used for chocolates. Instead, it was chock-full of packets of cigarettes, tobacco, cigarette papers, discarded bits of cheap jewelry, and, to quote Roy, "God knows what else. If you couldn't find anything, you would poke amongst it all." But Dad knew exactly where everything was, including the "overstock" in the two rooms on the upper floors.

The cash register was makeshift. "I'm not spending good money on newfangled machinery," Dad insisted, as he rummaged in a pullout drawer to make change. The drawer, kept under the counter, held three cardboard candy boxes for silver and copper coins and one- and five-pound notes. At the end of the fishing season and at Christmas time, there were plenty of ten-pound notes also. For Dad, these were "good days."

From the time I could look over the counter, I helped in the shop. Saturdays were the busiest days. Fishermen, going home for the weekend after five days at sea, stocked up on supplies, which included cases of beer and whisky, then visited Greenwald's, the only shop on the street selling condoms. Coming into the shop, they looked around furtively. "Is your Dad around?" Dad stopped whatever he was doing, pushing me out of the way. "How many?" he would ask, while groping deep into the back of the drawer, behind the boxes of silver and copper coins. With a magician's sleight of hand, he slipped half a dozen little foil packages into a brown paper bag. Money changed hands and everybody was happy. The fishermen were ready for the weekend at home.

January was a quiet time in the shop. Gales and driving rain forced the fishing boats to stay moored to the pier. People came in "just for a chat." Even if he had seen them the day before, Dad ushered good customers and friends into the back shop.

"Come in for a *dram*. It'll warm you up on this cold day." He had set up a tray with glasses, a bottle of the best whisky, and slices of Scribona cherry cake, purchased in a five-pound slab from Todds, the wholesalers. Dad didn't drink, but he joined in plenty of conversation and loud laughter.

In *simmer dim*, Greenwald's stayed open until nine or ten o'-clock at night. Hundreds of Dutch, Danish, and Norwegian fishermen came ashore for an hour or so. They also returned before they sailed at dawn. Ma remembered, "They were rowdy . . . banging on the shop door with their wooden clogs. I was afraid the door would be shattered. Of course, we threw on some clothes and opened the shop for them. They were in a hurry and bought Millers *pandrops* by the hundred-pound sack. Goodness knows what they did with it all. I suppose they sold it at a fine profit back home."

During the day, the shop door was always unlocked, even when Dad was upstairs. But the loud ringing of a bicycle bell attached to the top of the door announced every customer's entry. Dad took his time to finish whatever he was doing before going back to the shop. Until then, customers would wait patiently, looking through the piles of clothing and linens stacked up on shelves. Shetlanders are religious and, almost without exception, never stole anything. That was one of the Ten Commandments. The only murder had taken place more than one hundred years earlier, and it's not even certain that it was murder.

In 1937, Dad bought his first car from the wealthy owner of a herring station. The stations employed thousands of young women, who came from all over Scotland and Ireland to gut and pack the herring in barrels. Barrel makers were called coopers and they worked alongside the women, hammering wooden lids onto the filled barrels. Layers of coarse salt acted as a preservative, and the filled barrels were shipped to Eastern Europe and Russia.

On cold winter mornings, Dad had to coax the little red Austin—license number PS1136—to start by rotating an outer handle, "to loosen up the engine." Anticipating the heavy parcels he would load into the back, Dad took the car to MacTavish's garage.

"I need heavy-duty springs fitted onto the back of this car."

The mechanic, wiping greasy hands onto equally greasy overalls, asked, "Why? I'll vouch you can get a couple heavy men in the back and the car will take off like the wind."

Harry insisted. Springs were attached.

That same evening, he discussed new business plans with Jean. Grudgingly, he respected her business acumen.

"What do you think of renting the Cunningsburgh village hall to sell our goods? We could set it all out on those long tables they use for refreshments at the dances, and folk could come and look and buy. We wouldn't have to send orders out by bus anymore."

Jean figured this was another way to keep him away for a few days.

"That's a fine idea. Call it a sale. Advertise the date and time in *The Shetland Times*. And now you have the car, you'll be able to take more of everything."

Dad sent to the Scottish mainland to order more stock: striped dress shirts and fine wool underwear for the men, patterned silk blouses and skirts for the women. Ma looked on, without saying a word. "Not that he doesn't have enough in the stockrooms," she said later. "While he's gone, I'll have to move some of the clothing at a lower price to get rid of it."

On a bright summer morning, with puffy white clouds floating across a clear blue sky, Dad loaded the car and set off for the Cunningsburgh village hall. In spite of the heavy-duty springs, the tailgate was just an inch or two from the road's surface. Still, apart from stopping a few times to fill the radiator with water from nearby streams, he arrived in record time, with thick white fumes spurting from the exhaust pipe. He looked out in amazement. Scores of people were already milling around the front door. They had come on foot, motor bicycles, and pony.

Dad leaped out of the car. "What's going on? I need to get in. I'm having a sale here."

A couple of young men came forward. "We're here for the sale. Come on. We'll help you unload."

Dad was amazed. "I didn't know so many people would come."

Jim, one of the young men, replied, "If you come to us, it's not worth it to go to Lerwick or phone you to send out an order."

"This is just lovely," said old Chrissie, a *kishie* on her back. "I'm going to get pants and trousers for my old man—and maybe some knickers and a *peenie* for me. You'll see, this *kishie* will be full by the time I'm finished." She punched Dad playfully. "I'm first in line so don't you go serving the young lasses before me."

The sale was an enormous success, the first of weekly events in the country and the outlying islands. For Dad, these sales were social occasions as well as business transactions. Roars of laughter could be heard through the open doorway of the hall.

"Harry, do you need an assistant?" asked one young lass.

"Come on then," Dad shouted above the din, shoving a pile of brown paper and a roll of twine towards her, "start packing." From that time on, wherever he went, a young girl from the area helped at the sales. Dad's payment was "pick whatever you like." During the sales, Dad was always in charge of the money, which he kept in a leather pouch on a belt round his waist.

During the summer vacation, I was forced to help. "You can give them change," he told me. "But Dad," I wailed, "selling unfashionable, heavy underwear to country folk is no fun."

"Where do you think the money comes from to send you to college?"

College was my escape from Shetland. "What do you want me to do?"

Pointing to a bearded, wrinkled *crofter*, Dad replied,"Go help Danny find what he's looking for."

"He couldn't have sent me to take care of the Sandison boys," I muttered to myself. Tall, dark, and tanned from the wind and weather, the Sandison boys, jostling each other as they tried to enter the narrow doorway together, were my teenaged idols.

People were generous, and kept us well fed. One might bring a thermos of vegetable soup; someone else, fresh-baked soda scones stuffed with cold roast lamb; yet another, a jar of homemade pickled onions. And to go with the flasks of tea there was always a plate of what I called Crofter's Cookies. These could be anything from sweet, yeasty rolls, filled with butter cream, to crisp ginger cookies, depending on the location and who was the baker. "We just thought you might like something for your dinner." Dinner, which was at 1 P.M., was the highlight of my day. The soup was thick and savory; the *reestit* mutton—an old Shetland recipe of mutton steeped in salt water and then hung to dry and cure—imparted a smoky flavor; the scones were crusty on the outside and moist inside; and the hill-raised lamb was fresh-tasting, with just a hint of heather berries.

Ma stayed behind to tend the shop. "I'm not going to any sales," she announced. "I'm just happy to be left in peace." And her close women friends came over for cards, tea, and *kichel*.

JOHANN'S HEARTY RED LENTIL SOUP WITH DOUGHBOYS

SERVES 6

Though Johann used margarine, and vegetables were fresh from the garden, I take advantage of convenience products such as vegetable oil, prepared shredded vegetables, and a good canned beef broth.

2 tablespoons margarine or vegetable oil

1 large onion, thinly sliced

1 meaty marrowbone

2 teaspoons salt

4–5 peppercorns

2 bay leaves

8 cups water

2 teaspoons Bisto* or Worcestershire sauce

1 large carrot, shredded

1 small white turnip, peeled and diced

1 large potato, peeled and diced

$\frac{1}{2}$ cup red lentils, rinsed

$\frac{1}{2}$ cup snipped fresh parsley

In a large pot, heat the margarine or oil over medium heat. Add the onion and sauté 5 minutes or until soft. Add the marrowbone, salt, peppercorns, bay leaves, and water. Bring to simmer, skimming off the foam as it rises. Cover and cook for $1\frac{1}{2}$ hours.

Add the Bisto or Worcestershire sauce, carrot, turnip, potato, and lentils. Cover and simmer on low for 1 hour longer, or until vegetables are tender and potato is broken down. Stir often. Remove marrowbone. When it is cool enough to handle, dice the marrow and adhering meat (much of the meat will have fallen off the bone). Adjust seasoning. Just before serving, stir in the parsley.

*beef gravy mix, found in some supermarkets and British specialty stores

These fluffy potato dumplings are cooked on top of a thick soup or stew for a hearty, stick-to-the-ribs winter meal.

1 cup self-rising flour
$\frac{1}{2}$ teaspoon salt
scant $\frac{1}{4}$ teaspoon pepper
$\frac{1}{4}$ cup mashed potato
1 egg, lightly beaten
1 tablespoon chopped parsley
$\frac{3}{4}$ cup milk to mix

Place the flour, salt, and pepper in a medium bowl. Stir to mix. Make a well in center. Stir in the potato, egg, parsley, and enough milk to make a soft, sticky dough. Correct seasoning to taste. Drop by heaping tablespoonfuls onto simmering thick soups or stews. Cover and cook 10 minutes or until risen and cooked through.

PICKLED
ONIONS

2 pounds tiny white onions

4 cups water

½ cup kosher salt

½ teaspoon dried dill

6–8 whole cloves

1 quart English-style, malt vinegar

2 tablespoons pickling spice

4 bay leaves

Peel onions. Place in a medium heatproof bowl and set aside. In a medium pot, bring the water, salt, dill, and cloves to a boil. Pour over the onions. Cover and refrigerate overnight, or for 10 to 12 hours.

Place the vinegar, pickling spice, and bay leaves in a small saucepan. Cover and bring to simmer. Cook for 10 minutes.

Drain the liquid from the onions. Add onions to vinegar mixture. Cook, uncovered, for 15 minutes. Onions should still be firm, not soft. Transfer to hot, sterilized jars. Seal the jars. Allow to marinate for 3 to 4 weeks before using.

KICHEL

MAKES 24 TO 26 COOKIES

Ma used olive oil, but vegetable oil makes a lighter cookie.

3 eggs
3 tablespoons vegetable oil
$\frac{1}{2}$ cup sugar, divided
$\frac{1}{2}$ teaspoon almond flavoring
2 cups all-purpose flour
1$\frac{1}{2}$ teaspoons baking powder
$\frac{1}{2}$ teaspoon salt

Preheat oven to 375°F. Sprinkle a baking sheet lightly with flour. Set aside.

Whisk together the eggs, oil, 1 tablespoon sugar, and almond flavoring until light and foamy. Sift flour, baking powder, and salt together. Add gradually to egg mixture. Mix well.

Sprinkle half the remaining sugar on a board. Roll out dough on sugared board to about $\frac{1}{4}$-inch thickness. Sprinkle with remaining sugar. Cut into strips, about 2 x 4 inches. Place on prepared baking sheet. Bake in preheated oven 20 minutes, or until golden brown and slightly risen. Cool on wire tray.

56

Mackerel at Midnight

CROFTER'S
COOKIES

8 ounces (2 sticks) margarine

1½ cups dark brown sugar, packed

3 tablespoons golden syrup or honey

1 teaspoon ground ginger

3¼ cups quick-cooking oatmeal

Heat oven to 350°F. Spray a baking sheet with nonstick cooking spray.

In a saucepan, melt the margarine. Add the sugar, syrup or honey, and ground ginger, mixing to blend. Stir in the oatmeal. Mix well. Drop by heaped tablespoonfuls onto prepared baking sheet.

Bake in preheated oven for 15 minutes, or until edges are beginning to brown. Cool completely on a wire rack. Store in an airtight container.

6

Shetlanders: Lerwick's Characters

In Shetland, traditionally, young boys and men made their living from "going to the fishing," while women stayed home, tending the livestock and farming small plots of cabbages and potatoes. Before the discovery of oil off the Shetland Islands in the early 1970s, it was the custom for a family to buy their own fishing boat. All the men—father, husband, and married sons—would be at sea together, to keep the money in the family. But this was not always a good thing. Occasionally, during severe storms, a boat was lost at sea, and the men were swept overboard, their bodies never to be recovered. The women left behind were stoic, helped by an unwavering faith: "We just have to go on. . . . Surely the Lord must have a good reason for taking them." They labored on, single-handedly tending to the few sheep and hens, and planting turnips, cabbages, and potatoes. Neighbors kept them supplied daily with fish.

Women supplemented the family income by knitting the world-famous Shetland *jumpers*, gloves, and scarves, creating their own designs as they went along. Today, as then, girls learn to knit almost as soon as they can hold knitting needles. Teenagers, like their mothers, knit so quickly one can barely see the needles moving. Shetlanders have a unique method of knitting with four needles, so that items such as sweaters and socks are seamless. There is no need to sew pieces together. A leather knitting belt, with holes to anchor the fourth needle, is buckled around the waist and is still used today. The women were never idle. In the evening, after household chores were done, they sat around the peat fire, spinning wool from their sheep, knitting and chatting, stopping only for a few minutes to drink a cup of tea with a fresh baked *bannock*.

Lerwick was filled with colorful characters. Wilbert, bearded and unkempt, came from the island of Whalsay. Thus, everyone knew him as Whalsay Wilbert. His wife had been an accomplished seamstress and Wilbert a fine fiddler. After she died, Wilbert could be seen wandering the street on vague errands, with a scruffy little dog at his heels. In this caring community, concerned neighbors made sure he was fed and clothed, but took care never to make him feel he was "taking charity."

"Wilbert, I made too much soup today. Take this panful and heat it up for your dinner."

As Wilbert passed the bakery, Hector, the baker, yelled out, "Wilbert, glad to see you. Take this dozen rolls. It's the end of the day and I can't sell them."

And from a mother whose son had left to go whale hunting in the South Shetlands, "Please take this jacket and trousers. Robbie is away and grew out of this."

This sense of caring continues today. In the year 2000, when Russian fishermen—their boats stranded in Lerwick harbor—didn't have money to buy provisions, Shetlanders loaded up small motorboats, bringing sacks of potatoes, bread, lamb, and enough other staples to support them until the ship-owners finally sent funds.

Then there was Benny the Bellman, our neighbor. He lived in a one-room house at the top of the first flight of stone steps in Burns Lane. Benny had two jobs. "I can't live on what the Town Council doles out," he muttered to anyone who would listen. Each evening as darkness was falling, Benny strutted along Commercial Street, lighting the gas streetlights with a five-foot-long taper. If he overslept the next morning, the lights might not be extinguished until after the shops had opened and the street was busy with fishermen and housewives. And that only after an angry Lerwegian banged on his door.

"Benny, waken up, it's long past seven o'clock and the lights are still on! You won't be getting your *pay packet* this week what with the waste of gas."

Two weekly newspapers, *The Shetland Times* and *The Shetland News* (the latter now defunct), were published on Tuesdays and Fridays. On the days between, Benny, clanging a school bell, stood at the Market Cross, the center of Commercial Street, yelling out the current news of the day. "Hear ye, hear ye! There will be no milk at the

Hoversta dairy today. The launch cannot make it across the Bressay Sound." Or, "A purse containing some small change was found yesterday. Will the owner please go to Porteous' chemist shop and ask for Wilma." It was not twenty-first-century sensationalism, but passersby stopped to listen, hanging on to every word.

Ma had given up on getting kosher meat. The first batch she had ordered from the kosher butcher in Glasgow arrived at the end of a long hot sea journey, crawling with maggots.

"My God, the meat's being eaten alive," she screamed, tossing chops, roasts, and flanken into the trash can.

Ma decided, "There's no question . . . my children must have meat whether it is kosher or not. God will forgive me." However, in our house there was never any pork, shellfish, meat dishes cooked with milk, or milk and meat served at any one meal. Strictly adhering to these customs helped to give me a lifelong understanding of the laws of *kashrut*. Willie Mackay at Inkster's butcher shop quickly understood Ma's dietary rules for meat. Inkster's became the only butcher shop Ma would deign to step into.

I pestered Ma. "Can we go to the butcher shop today?" I loved leaving my footprints in the fresh sawdust that covered the floor, and listening to the good-natured banter.

"That's not good enough," Ma would say to Mr. Mackay as he offered a choice cut from the window. "Bring me something from the back." And he did.

"I've been saving this for the *bonniest* lady in Lerwick," he chuckled.

Ma shot back, "Am I not the *bonniest* in the whole of Shetland?"

"No, no," he replied. "You're the *bonniest* in Scotland."

Grasping my hand as we left the shop, she'd say, "They're all *meshuga* in this town except you and me, and I'm not so sure about you." To a five-year-old, this was hilarious and I giggled all the way home.

Eggs were as much a staple as flour and sugar. When Ma was in her late eighties, we told her about the dangers of cholesterol, but she pooh-poohed the idea. "Cholesterol be damned. I wouldn't be living this long if I didn't have a couple eggs every day . . . fresh-laid that is." (Ma died at ninety-two, bright and articulate until the end.)

In winter, eggs became scarce when production went down. Hubert, the egg man, who walked from his farm at Sound, a mile away, to make deliveries, would give us the news. "The hens aren't laying well. You'll have to learn to preserve eggs."

So Ma learned to preserve eggs. In summer, when they were plentiful, eggs were preserved by the water-glass method. A solution of sodium silicate and cooled, boiled water was poured into a clean, enamel bucket, until it was about one-third full. The fresh, unwashed eggs were arranged inside the bucket in layers, with about two inches of solution left above the final layer. The bucket was covered with a tight lid to prevent dust and insects from falling in, and then stored in a cool dark place, in the cellar or on a back porch. The liquid, which started out clear, gradually turned cloudy. Eggs preserved in this manner can be used for up to a year. Ours were eaten up by spring. We used a big wire-mesh strainer to scoop out as many eggs as we needed, always washing them first under cold, running water.

Hubert was full of advice. "The eggs have a natural sealer on the shell, so never wash them before putting them in the bucket and never serve them boiled."

Hubert made sure that he delivered the eggs mid-morning, when he knew Dad would be busy in the shop. Then he was free to flirt outrageously. Payment for a dozen eggs was one shilling, a cup of tea with plenty of sugar, and a thick slice of Ma's home-baked cake. Hubert was lavish with compliments.

"This is better than any oatcake in this world," he'd grin. "Where did you learn to bake like this? You could have a proper baker's shop."

"Och, you're a proper ladies' man," said Ma, blushing, as she slid another slice of caraway seed cake onto his plate, just as he'd hoped.

"Bring me two dozen tomorrow. It's Friday and I'm doing a big baking for the Sabbath."

We used at least a dozen eggs every day, giving Hubert legitimate reason for dropping in. We had pancakes or fried eggs for breakfast; eggs for cakes and rich cream scones; and, "to build us up for the winter," Ma's Coggly Woggly, a concoction of fresh eggs, whisked to a thick cream, with sugar, vanilla, and a tiny pinch of cinnamon.

Hubert's wife, Mabel, was annoyed and angry.

"You're going to the Greenwalds' again? You waste your time there drinking tea, and I have to hunt in the grass for the afternoon eggs."

"They don't eat bacon or pork, so they use a lot of eggs," he tried to explain. He didn't mention he liked sitting in Ma's kitchen just talking. "You're so interesting, having lived in the big city," he told her.

"Och, you're just a flatterer," she replied. Both enjoyed the attention lacking in their relationships with their spouses.

Poor, sad Tammie the Twirler lived at the top of Burns Lane, an object of pity. He was unable to walk in a straight line. Pale and thin, he walked two steps, then twirled around half a dozen more. This continued until he reached his destination. Even then, hopping from one foot to the other, he couldn't stand still. He talked with a stammer. If we had lived in a major city where he could have been treated by a neurologist, perhaps he would have been able to function with some degree of normalcy. As it was, Tammie lived out his days in a permanent state of confusion and frustration.

And there was Charlie Sandison, who, according to Dad, was "a double-crossing shyster . . . a black marketeer." You'd never guess they were the best of friends. You could hear them arguing and laughing whenever they were together. Charlie was a house painter. During World War II, food was strictly rationed. Each person was allowed only one pound each of sugar and butter per month, and many people hoarded coupons before clipping any from their ration books. But, each Saturday, Charlie appeared with a sheet-pan covered with a white cloth. Once in our kitchen, like a magician, he whipped the cloth away. The pan was crammed with yeast buns filled with sweet, whipped cream, little cakes covered with pink and white marzipan, red jam tarts, and butterfly cakes.

"Oooh, wow!" I exclaimed, eyes popping with excitement. "How many can I choose?"

"Just half a dozen. I have a lot of clients to visit yet," he explained.

All the clients, including Dad, cheerfully paid well for these precious luxuries at a time of austerity, never questioning the source.

COGGLY
WOGGLY

*Forget cholesterol! This sweet, creamy beverage was served to us
every winter morning, along with a plate of porridge in a
puddle of cream spooned from the top of the milk bottle.*

    1 fresh egg
    $\frac{1}{2}$ cup milk
    2 tablespoons sugar
    2 drops vanilla extract
    pinch cinnamon

Place all ingredients in a small bowl. Whisk with a fork, as Ma did,
until thick and creamy, or with an electric mixer. Serve immediately.

QUEEN OF HEARTS
JAM TARTS

MAKES 12

You can make the short-crust pastry in seconds in the food processor, or, as described below, you can do it the old-fashioned way: Cut margarine into dry ingredients until mixture resembles breadcrumbs. Add enough water to make a stiff dough.

3 cups all-purpose flour
1 tablespoon sugar
pinch salt
1 1/4 sticks (10 tablespoons) margarine
5–6 tablespoons ice water to mix
red fruit preserves and lemon curd or apricot preserves

Preheat oven to 400°F. Spray a tray of muffin tins with nonstick cooking spray.

Place flour, sugar, and salt in food-processor bowl, fitted with steel blade. Pulse once or twice to mix. Cut margarine in 10 pieces and add. Process until mixture resembles fine breadcrumbs. Add enough ice water to form a ball. Turn onto a floured board.

Roll pastry out thinly. Using a 3-inch, fluted cookie cutter, cut in rounds. Place each round in one of the prepared muffin cups. Place a teaspoonful of red preserves in 6 pastry-lined cups, then a teaspoonful of lemon curd or apricot preserves in remaining cups. Cut small hearts out of any leftover pastry. Place on top of preserves, one on each tart.

Bake in preheated oven for 15 minutes, or until edges are golden brown. If desired, fill tarts with extra preserves when cooked.

BUTTERFLY CAKES

We called these butterfly cakes, as the muffin tops, cut in half, resembled butterfly wings.

CAKE
1 cup all-purpose flour
2 teaspoons baking powder
1 stick (4 ounces) butter, softened
$\frac{1}{2}$ cup sugar
2 eggs
$\frac{1}{2}$ teaspoon vanilla extract

BUTTER CREAM
4 tablespoons butter, softened
1 cup confectioners sugar
2 teaspoons milk or cream as needed

confectioners sugar to dust

Preheat oven to 350°F. Place 9 paper muffin cases in a muffin cup tray. Stir the flour and baking powder together. Set aside.

Place butter and sugar in a bowl. Beat until pale and fluffy. Add 1 egg and 2 tablespoons of the flour mixture. Beat well to mix. Beat in vanilla and remaining egg with 2 more tablespoons of the flour mixture. Add remaining flour gradually, scraping down the sides of the bowl. Spoon batter into muffin cases, filling each about three-quarters full.

Bake in preheated oven 18 to 20 minutes, or until risen and firm in center (cake should spring back when lightly pressed with finger). Cool on a wire rack and prepare Butter Cream.

Butter Cream: Whip butter until pale. Gradually stir in confectioners sugar. Add enough milk or cream to make a spreading consistency.

To assemble: Cut a slice from the top of each cake, then cut each slice in half, crosswise. Spoon a little butter cream on cut surface of each cake. Insert two halves of slices on each surface to resemble wings. Dust lightly with confectioners sugar.

7

Life in the Lane

Ma was the parent who instilled a proud Jewish identity in her children. She had attended *cheder* and could read Hebrew fluently until the end of her life. When she celebrated Passover with us, family and friends marveled at how effortlessly she read the *Haggadah*. Living in Shetland, we were unable to attend Hebrew school, the nearest being more than two hundred miles away, across an ocean. Neither Ma nor Dad had a spare minute to teach us. Ma shopped, cooked, cleaned, and cared for her family. Dad ran the shop and each week, laden with packages, went to the country to sell clothing and jewelry. Ma was left to take care of customers in the shop, along with her other chores.

Still, in spite of our isolation, Ma was determined to retain her Jewishness and pass on its rich heritage and culture to her children. From the moment I could talk, I knew I was Jewish and that we did some things differently from our neighbors. When I was four years old, playing hide and seek with Edith, Granny Hunter's teenaged daughter, she called out, "Who is this *peerie* lass that I can't find?" Instead of answering, "I'm Ethel," when I crawled out from under the table, I answered emphatically, "I'm here, and I'm a British Jew."

I learned not so much by what Ma said, but by her example. Though the shop was open on Saturdays, we didn't write or do laundry or any other unnecessary work. Ma was up early on Friday morning to prepare for the Sabbath. The kitchen was a hive of activity. Cathy, the daily help, spent the morning cleaning. Under Ma's close supervision, my grandmother's brass, rope-like candlesticks were polished until they sparkled; newspapers spread over the freshly scrubbed floor would not be picked up until just before lighting the Sabbath candles at dusk. Her hands over her eyes, Ma whispered the age-old blessing.

Shabbat was a much anticipated feast. Dairy meals were easy to prepare, for there was an abundance of fish, eggs, milk, and butter. There were platters of fried gefilte fish sprinkled with malt vinegar and salt, a method Ma picked up, and liked, from the corner fish and chip shop. Poached gefilte fish balls were garnished with slices of carrot. Bowls of pickled herring were draped with fronds of dill and bay leaves. Herring was also chopped with a *messer* on a wooden board and mixed with hard-boiled eggs, vinegar, onions, and a crust of brown bread. The rye bread Ma had used in Glasgow was unavailable in Shetland. A three-tiered, silver cake stand held slices of strudel and *mandelbrot*.

Food was important not just as a means of survival, but also because, as Ma repeatedly told me, "it's made with love that makes it taste so good." As a toddler, perched on a chair, I watched each step of preparation with admiration. "Ma," I remember telling her, "you make the best meals." She beamed. "You will do it, too, and maybe even better than me."

"No," I said seriously, shaking my head. "I don't think so."

As soon as I could reach the table by kneeling on a chair, Ma allowed me to help. She broke off a chunk of short-crust pastry from the batch she had made.

"Sprinkle a little flour and then this is how you roll it out," she said, guiding my pudgy little hands on the miniature wooden rolling pin. Patiently, we baked step by step. "Now you press the top of the glass down and cut it into circles."

Greasing the baking pan was fun.

"Crumple up a piece of greaseproof paper, dip it into the melted butter, and then wipe it around the pan. Then lay your pastry on top, and we'll put it in the oven to bake along with the other cakes and cookies." We placed my "biscuits" on a baking sheet. When they were baked, I spread each one with jam and passed them round at teatime. I must say, Ma and Dad gamely nibbled on these morsels, pronouncing them "delicious."

Ma's cooking was Ashkenazi. I was convinced we ate much better than our neighbors. In Shetland, boiling or frying were the standard cooking methods for fish, but Ma cooked fish in a dozen different ways, such as baked mackerel with gooseberry sauce, and grilled *finnan haddie* with a knob of butter and minced garlic. Though I never refused home-baked scones, oatcakes, or *brunnies* at my playmates' houses, Ma's strudels stuffed with apples and raisins, crunchy sugar-crusted *kichel*, and scoops of her creamy "dripped" cheese, crowned with dollops of rhubarb-and-fig jam, were in my opinion vastly superior.

Dad may not have been happy in his marriage, but he was delighted and satisfied with Ma's cooking. He ate selectively (you might have called him a picky eater), but he loved to eat. He didn't like sauces or gravy, which Shetlanders made with Bisto, a beef gravy mix. "I don't cook like that anyway," she said. "Bisto is not kosher." He liked newly dug-up potatoes from "the Ness," the south part of the Mainland, the largest of the Shetland Islands, where the soil yields a mealy, dark-skinned variety. Each autumn, Dad bought a hundred-pound sack. No one talked about vitamins leaching out into the cooking water, but when Ma cooked vegetables—carrots, turnips, and cabbage—her inner intuition made her save the cooking liquids for our soups, which she made every day, summer or winter.

Dad always got up early so that he could have plenty of time in the bathroom. Obsessively clean and neat, he washed his hands frequently, especially before touching any food and after packing each parcel in the shop. Before mouthwash flooded the market, Dad gargled each morning with a solution of aspirin and warm water. Then he stoked up the fire, lugging in two buckets of peat to set at the fireside. In the Shetland home, during World War II, there was always a warm fire. Every family had their own peat stacked at the side of the house.

Dad cooked his own breakfast, rationalizing, "I make it the way I like it." It was consistent and spare. He had two slices of whole-wheat toast, scraping the excess butter off to leave just a film. Because he liked his tea weak and pale, Ma poured him the first cup before it had time to brew. He never added milk or sugar. "Gives it a strange taste," he said. Thick, coarse porridge was stirred with the *spurtle*. Milk was not homogenized and came from the cow to the containers. A two-inch-thick layer of cream always floated to the top of the milk bottle. Dad ate his porridge with milk, "but first pour off the cream for the *kinder*." We were extremely well fed on pure whole foods; and when cholesterol became the negative buzzword, according to Ma, "Never you mind. If you can't enjoy your food, life's not worth living."

We always sat down together at mealtimes, but Friday night was special. First, Ma said the blessing over the candles; Dad made *kiddush* with sweet, syrupy wine poured into a little silver cup. I was given a sip. Instead of our usual high tea, including sardines on toast or baked beans and sausages, we dined on chicken soup, with *knaid-*

lach, and roast chicken, typical of Sabbath dinners served all over Eastern Europe. After such a meal, Dad, licking his lips, lapsed into Yiddish—"a *meichle,* a truly wonderful meal"—a rare compliment to Ma.

Dad didn't work on Friday evening. Instead, he lifted his violin from its worn case lined with threadbare red velvet and played lively but nonsensical tunes, humming along. These were the rare times he appeared lighthearted and happy. Sadly, his music wasn't appreciated.

"That's enough," Ma would say as she brought out Ludo, and Snakes and Ladders. "What color counter do you want?"

We played the games together until it was time for "nine o'clocks," when we paused for a tea break. Everything stopped for tea and hot, buttered toast. We took turns toasting thick slices of Malcolmson's bread over glowing coals. Lacking an electric toaster, we used a toasting fork with a long adjustable handle. As soon as the bread was nicely browned, we rushed to slather each slice with butter, so we could eat it with the melted butter dripping down our chins. Then it was time for bed.

"Tomorrow is a work day for some of us," Ma would say, reminding us that "there's no writing or sewing to be done. Homework will be done on Sunday." Business was brisk on Saturdays, and to close the shop for the Sabbath would have meant financial ruin.

During the week, when I came home from school, Ma was always in the kitchen waiting for me with a mug of steaming Horlicks, a malt drink, and a wedge of apple strudel. Latchkey kids were in the far-off future.

Ma was beginning to gather a group of close friends around her and had joined the Eastern Star and SWRI (Scottish Women's Rural Institute), a women's group dedicated to home and hearth. They held competitions for the best knitwear, baking, jams, and preserves. Ma's specialties were jams, particularly rhubarb and black currant. Rhubarb grew along the roadsides and in gardens, multiplying each year. Ma was creative. She added chopped, dried figs or dates to her rhubarb jam. No one ever needed to persuade her to enter any of the competitions. "I know I have a superior product. Everybody uses cloves and crystallized ginger. Mine is different." And she proudly walked away with prizes. If she didn't win, she attributed it to favoritism.

"Humph! That woman is the judge's mother-in-law"; or, "she took the recipe from last month's *Woman's Own* magazine. Wouldn't you say that's plagiarism?"

For Shetland women, summer was a happy, busy time. The scent of bubbling sugar and fruit wafted through the hallway down to the shop. Besides rhubarb jam and chutneys and black currant preserves, Ma made strawberry jam. When the boat docked from Aberdeen bringing the weekly supplies, Dad was first in line at Herriott's, the fruit importer. "I'll take all the strawberries if you give me a good price."

Delighted to get rid of the stock, which, unrefrigerated, would quickly become completely spoiled, Herriott's agreed on a deal. And Dad carried twelve pints of overripe strawberries back to the shop.

Ma wailed, "How much strawberry jam can I make? Without lemons, it never sets properly and I can't even give it away. It certainly won't win any prizes at the Lerwick competition." That was until she hit on the idea of presenting it as strawberry sauce, another resounding family winner.

Jam making was a two-day process. It began in mid-summer, when rhubarb is less acid and black currants are plump and juicy. Every housewife made her own version of rhubarb jam. But the basic recipe was the same: one pound of rhubarb to one pound of sugar. Rhubarb was free for the picking; all you had to add was sugar.

First, the dark-green, fanlike leaves were cut away from the red stems. Flinging the leaves into the sink, Ma was dramatic in her warnings. "The green is poisonous, oxalic acid; you can die if just one shred goes into the pan." Terrified, I kept a watchful eye on the pan.

"Ma, I don't want to die."

Ma was always practical. She handed me a slotted metal spoon. "Just fish out anything green."

Using her sharpest knife and the scrubbed wooden board, she cut the stems into neat half-inch lengths. Ma explained everything as she went along, for "some day you'll want to be making this jam."

"First, we weigh the rhubarb," she said, tipping the pieces onto the brass pan on the scale. "We should have about seven pounds." She scooped sugar out of a bin. "Then add seven pounds sugar. Now all we have to do is mix the sugar and rhubarb together and let it rest."

I stood on a chair so that I could reach the jelly pan, and Ma gave me a long-handled wooden spoon. "Now, you can stir for a bit."

We covered the pan with a clean white cloth and left it on the kitchen counter overnight. Next day, the sugar had liquefied, and the rhubarb, floating in a sugar "brine," had changed from bright crimson to dull red. Ma chopped a heap of dried figs into tiny pieces. "You stir and I'll pour them in."

The pan, now heavy with the rhubarb mixture, was lifted onto the stove. As the mixture began to simmer, Ma skimmed off the foam. "That's all the impurities. If that's mixed in we'll have a cloudy jam—and that won't win any prizes."

After simmering on the stove for an hour or so, it was ready. Testing was rather primitive but it worked. The perfect spoonful of jam, when poured onto a saucer, jelled in a minute or two. Clean jars from last year's batch had been sterilized in the oven, "baked" at the lowest temperature. The hot mixture was ladled into the jars. Then the final step: Melted paraffin wax was poured over the tops to make tight seals, and the covers were screwed on. We attached labels to the jars, with the names of the jams and the dates they had been made, then stored the jars in the coolest place in the house, the cellar under the shop.

At the end of summer, jams and jellies and mustard pickles—all in jars of assorted shapes and sizes—were arranged neatly on two long shelves. It was important that all were *pareve*, so they could be served with dairy or meat meals. Ma stood back and proudly surveyed her work. "I've bottled the best of summer. Isn't that chust lovely?"

Dad was "in the trade," so Ma divided her time between flat and shop. Her days were a frenzy of cleaning, cooking, and attending to customers. She would dash up and down the wooden stairs. "I should be thin as a rake, with all this running up and down," she puffed.

With each of her two pregnancies, she had continued to gain weight. Dad's scorn—"You're too fat"—and eating what I had left on my plate, along with the starchy Shetland diet, didn't help. Lettuce, radishes, cucumbers, and fruit were only available in summer. In winter, fresh produce couldn't survive the unrefrigerated journey from England to Shetland. And she, along with her friends, found it impossible to give up the frequent cups of tea and chocolate biscuits. With Ma, it was partly frustration. With her friends, it was gluttony.

Dad believed in buying in bulk. In fact it was an obsession, possibly a carryover from growing up in Gorodea, where food was scarce and expensive when available. "I want to be sure you all have plenty to eat," he said. "Bread must be fresh from the baker's every day, and whatever's leftover we can toss to the gulls." The birds swooped down on whatever scraps were thrown out, and there were plenty. At Todds, the wholesalers, Dad carted home five-pound slabs of cakes, his favorites: sultana and cherry, manufactured by Scribona and shipped to Shetland. Ma cut each slab into one-pound pieces. "We're never going to eat all this before it gets stale," she would sigh as she packed it into a big square tin. I agreed. "Ma, I like your cakes better."

Putting her arm around me, she smiled."I know that. You're a good wee lass."

Eventually, the cake was crumbled and we tossed it out into the back yard. Swarms of screaming gulls swooped down, and, in seconds, not a crumb was left.

Ma's mantra, "cleanliness is next to godliness," was not easy to keep. Vacuum cleaners did not exist. Women carried rugs outside, threw them over a line, then beat the heck out of them with a flat, cane whisk. Living above the shop, we had no yard; so, instead, we pushed a carpet sweeper that sucked up the dust into a container. Monday was washday, a long, arduous chore. Even the latest contraption, a hand-operated Jiffy washing machine, didn't make it easier. Buckets of water were heated on the stove, then Ivory Snow soap flakes poured into the machine. Ma pushed the metal arm that agitated the clothes until she was satisfied they were clean. Each week, as long as it wasn't raining, Ma heaved the tub of heavy, wet wash onto her hip and plodded up the lane to the communal drying green, where neighbors took turns hanging their wash out to dry. If the weather was wet and sleety, on coming home, we'd find clothes festooned around the fireplace, on the rungs of a wooden pulley strung up on the ceiling, and hung over the backs of chairs.

Eventually they dried, albeit stiffly. In sunny weather, bed linen was spread on the grass to bleach in the sun. I was never aware of grass stains. More often than not, Dad was in the country; so Ma soldiered on, with occasional help from Cathy.

MA'S CREAMY
"DRIPPY" CHEESE

We called it "drippy cheese" because the soured milk, caught in a large linen handkerchief, was hung over the sink to drip off the liquids. Two of the best Irish linen men's handkerchiefs from the shop were stored in a drawer, and kept specifically for cheese making. My frugal grandmother handed the recipe down to Ma.

"Let the milk (about 2 cups) stand overnight at room temperature, to become curdled and sour. Add a tablespoonful of vinegar to hasten the process. Take a large, Irish linen handkerchief, and tie a string loosely around the four corners to make a pouch. Pour the soured milk in, pull the corners together, and tie tightly, leaving a loop. Hang over the kitchen faucet, so that liquids can drip into the sink. Leave overnight. The contents will have solidified. Turn into a dish, scraping all the cheese from the handkerchief folds. Mash with a fork and season with pepper and salt. The cheese will keep in a cold place for 2 to 3 days."

The texture was between cottage and cream cheese. No preservatives were added. Tangy and peppery, this was homemade, pure, soft cheese at its finest.

RHUBARB, FIG,
AND GINGER JAM

MAKES 8 TO 10 PINTS

*Shetlanders made rhubarb jam spiked with ginger or cloves.
Ma added chopped figs or slivered dates to her recipe.*

4 pounds rhubarb stems, cut in $\frac{1}{2}$-inch slices

4 pounds granulated sugar

6 ounces crystallized ginger

1$\frac{1}{2}$ tablespoons powdered ginger

$\frac{3}{4}$ pound dried figs, chopped, or 1 pound dates,
stones removed, each cut into 8 slivers

Place rhubarb, sugar, crystallized ginger, and powdered ginger in a
large nonmetallic bowl. Stir gently to mix. Cover and leave at room
temperature for 24 hours.

Pour off the liquid into a preserving pan or large, heavy-bottomed
pot. Bring to a boil. Add the rhubarb, gingers, figs, or dates. Return
to a boil. Skim off any foam. Reduce to simmer. Cook for 45 minutes
longer, or until a spoonful of jam jells when dribbled onto a cool
saucer.

Pour into sterilized jars. Cover and seal. Label with name of jam and
the date. Store in a cool, dry place.

RHUBARB CHUTNEY

1 medium onion, cut in chunks

2½ cups sliced rhubarb

½ cup brown sugar, packed

⅓ cup white vinegar

2 tablespoons water

1 teaspoon salt

1 teaspoon dry mustard

¼ teaspoon each, cinnamon and ground cloves

⅓ cup raisins

¾ cup chopped dates

Place the onion and rhubarb in a food processor. Pulse 5 to 8 seconds until chunky; pieces should be about ¼-inch in size. Set aside. In a large, heavy saucepan over medium heat, mix the sugar, vinegar, water, salt, mustard, cinnamon, and cloves. Bring to a boil, stirring to dissolve the sugar. Reduce heat to simmer and cook 2 to 3 minutes.

Stir in the chopped onion and rhubarb. Cover; bring to a boil. Reduce heat and simmer 15 minutes. Add the raisins and dates. Continue cooking, covered, for 10 minutes or until thick. Stir often. Spoon into jars. Store in refrigerator for up to 4 weeks.

PEPPERED HADDOCK PASTE

Fish and meat pastes are still popular sandwich fillings in Shetland, served at church teas along with trays of fancies. Shrimp was often used, but Ma substituted cooked hake or salmon. May also be served with melba toast.

2 cups cooked salmon, skin and bones removed
6 tablespoons melted butter or margarine
1 teaspoon anchovy paste
1 teaspoon Worcestershire sauce
pinch ground mace
tiny pinch cayenne pepper

In a bowl, mash the salmon to a paste (may be done in the food processor). Beat in 4 tablespoons of the melted butter or margarine, anchovy paste, Worcestershire sauce, mace, and cayenne. Transfer to a small serving dish. Pour the remaining butter or margarine over the paste. Serve chilled.

MAKES 30 PIECES

Instead of working the sugar and butter into the flour by hand, a laborious process, Ma prepared it her own way. This method is easy, buttery, and melts in the mouth.

1 cup unsalted butter, at room temperature
½ cup plus 1 tablespoon sugar, divided
½ teaspoon almond extract
2 cups all-purpose flour
⅓ cup dried currants

Preheat oven to 350°F. Grease a 9-inch-square baking dish with butter or spray with nonstick cooking spray.

In a bowl, beat the butter and ½ cup sugar until light and fluffy. Add the almond extract, then the flour gradually, about ⅓ cup at a time. With a spoon, work in the currants. Press mixture into prepared dish. Sprinkle with remaining sugar.

Bake in preheated oven until edges are beginning to turn golden, about 25 minutes. Cut hot shortbread into squares. Cool completely to serve.

8

The War Years: 1939 to 1945

My brother Roy was born on a wild February night, in 1941. Gale-force winds lashed hailstones against the windowpanes, and because of the blackout, there were no streetlights. The ambulance carrying Ma to the cottage hospital moved slowly under cover of darkness.

We had been issued gas masks, but, for babies, zippered, rubber, boatlike contraptions—similar to a little closed bassinet—were distributed. "We'll all be blown to pieces if we take the time to lay Roy into this," Ma said scornfully. The masks smelled of rubber, and a little baby would be kicking and screaming to get out. Thankfully, the only time we had to use them was during emergency drills, and then it was just for a minute or two.

I was three years old when the first rumblings of the atrocities taking place in Europe were heard. At five o'clock, teatime, my parents shooed me into a corner as they huddled over the radio. So that I wouldn't hear the grim news of Jews being sent to labor camps, I was told, "Go make tea for your teddy bear." Not really understanding, but knowing that something very frightening was taking place—events that might invade and wreck my small, safe world—I obediently set out treasured, miniature, green glass cups and saucers.

We were Jews. Anxious and apprehensive, my parents whispered to each other in Yiddish, so that I wouldn't understand. However, I grew to understand every word. They voiced their fears.

"Maybe we should take down the sign over the shop."

"No, we have good friends here . . . if we must, we'll leave everything and just vanish."

Four-year-old Ethel, in Gilbertson
Park

It seemed to me that young men who had been our neighbors
suddenly disappeared. *Drafted* became a common word. Old men who
stayed behind spent long hours in our shop. They were convinced "it'll
all be over in a few weeks. Our boys will wipe those bloody Huns off
the face of the earth. . . . They'll come back heroes!"

My parents were not so confident. Dad had escaped from the
brutality of pogroms. Ma had experienced the taunts of anti-Semitism
at school, all but forgotten now that she lived in Shetland. News
reached us of the Germans marching triumphantly northwards to
Scandinavia. Each day brought new developments in what now had become anticipation of a long war. Barbed wire was hurriedly unrolled to
create eight-foot-high double fences along the pier and shore to protect the town. Enormous concrete blocks, the size of small cottages,
were placed inland to halt enemy tanks. Battleships were anchored in
the harbor. Hundreds of soldiers arrived daily, rifles over their shoulders, marching in formation down the gangway leading from the decks
of long, gray battleships anchored alongside Victoria Pier. Hustled onto
buses, they were driven to Nissen huts, prefabricated shelters with cor-
rugated iron roofing and concrete floors, hastily erected all over the
Mainland of Shetland. In Lerwick, air-raid shelters—windowless, dark,

cavelike structures—were strategically placed so that everyone could reach them in a matter of minutes.

Shetland was an important and essential naval base. Because of its deep, natural harbor, the Germans targeted Lerwick. From there, the enemy could have control of the North Sea and the Atlantic Ocean. In a lonely house on the island of Lunna, one of the Allied forces' secret headquarters, massive military operations were planned. It's alleged that the German spy, Rudolf Hess, was imprisoned there until he was moved to more secure quarters in England.

Almost six hundred years ago, Shetland belonged to Norway, and the story goes that at least 60 percent of the Shetland population carry the genes of Norwegian Vikings. With Norway now under German occupation, and so near the islands, Shetlanders, out of fear and hatred of the enemy, wholeheartedly manned the "Shetland Bus": a fleet of small fishing vessels that, under cover of darkness, made perilous journeys across the North Sea to bring refugees and resistance fighters from Norway to the safety of the Shetland Islands. "Taking the Shetland Bus" was the code for escape. It was so successful that the German army received top-priority orders from Berlin that the Shetland Bus must be stopped and destroyed.

The siren's wail signaled the approach of enemy planes. One flew so low over Lerwick that the pilot—wearing goggles and helmet—could be seen in the cockpit, and the swastika, painted on the tail. Douglas, a peace-loving *crofter*, ran outside with his World War I rifle, firing shots into the fuselage. The plane exploded and plunged into the harbor.

"Ha! Got the bloody bugger," he said, adding, "yes, I'm peace-loving, but those German bastards are killers of women and children." From every corner of the islands, Douglas was immediately hailed as a man of distinguished valor. He was interviewed and photographed for *The Shetland Times*, the headline proclaiming, "Our National Hero!" For the rest of his life, he was "the man who shot down the Hun."

Our air-raid shelter was only a hundred yards away, down by the pier. Even so, by the time we had grabbed flashlights and gas masks, run downstairs in nightclothes and along the street, the all-clear had sounded. Each day, I walked with my schoolmates to kindergarten. Ma sent me off with a hug and a kiss and my gas mask in a brown cardboard box slung over my shoulder. When the sirens went off, teachers marched us into the air-raid shelter at the bottom of the playground. Hiding their fear, they kept us occupied and amused.

"Let's sing about the hole in the bucket."

After singing several songs, we grew impatient. "Miss Petrie, what can we do now?"

The elderly spinster teacher had years of experience keeping little ones busy. "Who would like to start to tell a story?"

And, even in those days of strict rationing, we passed cookies and milk around.

We were never in the shelters for more than an hour. When the all-clear sounded, we rushed out into the fresh air. Bombs had not fallen. We were safe. To us children, the air raid didn't seem so bad; it was more like an adventure.

The radio was our only means of communication with the outside world. The news from the front was discouraging, blaring out across the airwaves twenty-four hours a day. Winston Churchill addressed us constantly, urging the "Brits" to fight to the bitter end: "We will be victorious." Young and old hung on to his every word. The Germans had advanced into Norway, about two hundred miles across the North Sea from Shetland. Dad's sullen, silent moods were less frequent. He and Ma, painfully aware of potential danger, as the only Jewish family in Shetland, threw their energies into the war effort. Dad helped organize the Home Guard, a contingent of shopkeepers, farmers, and others not eligible for duty, who patrolled the streets after dark. It was essential that all windows and doors be completely covered with thick blinds. He led them on in his mixture of Yiddish and Shetland dialect. "Let's go lads—we cannot let a *kleine licht* be seen." It worked. The few bombs targeted for Lerwick fell into the sea.

In spite of the strain or how bad the weather was, Ma was always singing. "Och, what's the point of being down? As long as we can laugh and sing, how bad can it be?" In Yiddish, she sang "My Yiddishe Momma" and "Rozinkes and Mandlen," the latter as she dished up a bowl of almonds and raisins "for the *bairns* to snack on." By the time I was five, I was singing, word-perfectly, the Yiddish and Scottish songs Ma had grown up with. As Harry Lauder, the most popular tenor of that time, belted out "Bonnie Dundee" and "I love a Lassie" on the radio, Ma and I would sing along at the tops of our voices. "There's nothing like the old Scottish songs," she would say.

During the war, the military men and women far outnumbered the Shetland population. More than three hundred Jewish soldiers were stationed in Shetland at any given time, and the Greenwald kitchen above the shop was a gathering place for them. The kitchen

Mackerel at Midnight

was small, but when half a dozen young airmen sat in the corner arm-chairs and three or four army corporals lounged on the sofa, it was cozy and cheerful. For a few hours, these young men and women could be carefree. After Shetland, they might be posted to the war front. Ma had only one rule. "No smoking. I can't have this fog in here. It's not healthy and Ethel won't be able to breathe. She'll get asthma." That didn't keep them away. They could meet other Jews, and the con-versation—in English, with heavy doses of Yiddish and Glaswegian—was loud and animated. At the Greenwalds', they felt at home.

Ma always had a pot of chicken soup and *knaidlach*, simmering on the back of the stove. In spite of strict rationing, she managed to cook up copious amounts of blintzes, strudels, and *kugels*, all the dishes they had enjoyed "before this bloody war." This would not have been possible if it had not been for the generous gifts of tea, butter, and sugar, spirited away from the camp kitchens by soldiers who looked on the Greenwald house as their second home.

"They sit here till the wee hours," said Ma, but she never com-plained. "The poor souls are away from home, and who knows if they'll ever return."

During the war years, the shop was busier than ever, and both my parents worked long hours. Sales were complicated. Each person was allowed only a certain number of clothing coupons. For each piece of clothing sold, the appropriate number of coupons were cut out of ration books and sent in to a central office. Help was hired for the shop and house—young, single women clamoring "to work for the Greenvalds." The attraction? At any time of the day or evening, a dozen young soldiers would find their way to Greenwald's shop or to the flat above the shop. Saturday night dances were held on the camp bases, and our girls flirted outrageously to wangle an invitation.

"Mrs. Greenvald, is it OK to go upstairs and put on my makeup?"

Ma was predictable, chuckling, "Lasses, just go and have a good time. And don't do anything I wouldn't do!"

On these evenings, our bedroom was the scene of elaborate preparations. I watched, wide-eyed. To me, the girls getting ready to go to the dance were glamorous and dazzling. They shared lipstick, coloring their lips and rubbing a little into their cheeks instead of rouge. The brighter the red the better—one shade for all and they were lucky to get it. Dresses, which had been sewn from the white and cream silk salvaged from downed parachutes, were clinging and sen-suous. As for silk stockings, Dad scolded his young customers, "There are none to be had. Don't you know silk is needed for the war effort?"

No problem. Legs smeared with tanning lotion were instantly bronzed, and a moistened eyebrow pencil carefully drawn down the back of each leg created the dark seam, the height of prewar fashion. There was good-natured jostling to get in front of the mirror hanging on the back of the door.

The final touch was a whiff of Evening in Paris. I was allowed to pass around the dark-blue perfume bottle and I didn't want them to forget about me.

"Who has the Evening in Paris?"

"Oops, almost forgot."

They handed me the bottle with a warning. "Careful now. We've spent the last of our coupons this month. That bottle has to last us a long time."

I was fascinated. A little dab behind each ear, then behind each knee, and a bit more in the deep cleavage exposed by a daringly low neckline.The young women streamed downstairs, throwing on coats, scarves, and gloves as they ran.

I was thrilled. "Cheerio, you all look so *bonnie*," and, picking up on their chatter, "you'll be sure to get a lad tonight."

We all had to make do with the clothes we had. This was especially difficult for parents of growing children. As I grew taller, Ma lengthened coats and skirts by inserting a wide strip of material from another garment above the hems. She made sure that the strip coordinated with the rest of the garment. Dark brown from an old woolen dress was used to lengthen my velvet-collared, brown tweed coat—an instant fashion statement.

BEST SWEET AND
SOUR CABBAGE SOUP

When the Jewish soldiers brought Ma a precious package of brown sugar, it came with a request for her famous cabbage soup. For ease and speed, I use packaged, shredded coleslaw mix. Chop onions in the food processor or, in a pinch, use frozen chopped onions.

2 tablespoons olive oil
2 large onions, coarsely chopped
1 teaspoon salt
3 tablespoons beef bouillon granules
1 (16 ounce) package coleslaw mix
1 (46 ounce) can tomato juice
1 (14½ ounce) can chopped tomatoes
4 bay leaves
juice of 2 large lemons
½ cup brown sugar, or to taste
white pepper to taste

In an 8-quart pot, heat the oil over medium heat. Add the onions and salt. Stir and cover. Cook over low heat for 30 minutes or until soft and golden. Stir in the bouillon and coleslaw mix. Cover. Cook over low heat 30 minutes.

Add the tomato juice, canned tomatoes, 1½ cups water, bay leaves, lemon juice, and brown sugar. Stir. Season to taste with white pepper. Partially cover and simmer 40 minutes longer. Add a little more brown sugar if desired. Remove bay leaves before serving.

FRIED
GEFILTE FISH

Ma always threw in a bit of hake: "Makes it sweeter," she maintained, but any white-fleshed fish may be used. A food processor makes this quick and easy.

1 pound haddock fillets

½ pound hake fillets

1 small onion cut in chunks

1 small scallion, green part only

2 eggs

2 teaspoons sugar

2 teaspoons salt

scant ¼ teaspoon white pepper

½ to ¾ cup matzo meal, plus more to coat

vegetable oil for frying

malt vinegar to sprinkle

Cut fish into 2-inch pieces. Place in a food processor. Add onion and pulse until coarsely chopped. Add the scallion and pulse to chop coarsely. Transfer to a bowl. Stir in the eggs, sugar, salt and pepper, and enough matzo meal to form a soft but workable mixture. With wet hands, shape into oval patties about ¾-inch thick. Dredge in additional matzo meal to coat on both sides.

Heat oil 1-inch deep in a large, heavy skillet. Fry patties over medium heat, turning once, until nicely browned on both sides, about 6 minutes total. Drain on paper towels. Sprinkle with malt vinegar. Serve at room temperature.

HONEY LOCKSHEN KUGEL

MAKES 15 TO 18 SERVINGS

6 eggs

1 cup light cream

1 1/2 cups milk

1/4 cup sugar

6 tablespoons margarine, melted and divided

3 tablespoons honey, warmed and divided

2 teaspoons cinnamon

1/8 teaspoon powdered cloves

1 cup dark raisins

2 apples, peeled and grated coarsely

1 pound vermicelli, cooked and drained

Preheat oven to 350°F. Butter an 11 x 13-inch baking dish or spray with nonstick cooking spray.

In a large bowl, whisk the eggs, cream, milk, sugar, 4 tablespoons melted margarine, 2 tablespoons honey, cinnamon, and cloves. Stir in the raisins, grated apples, and vermicelli. Transfer to prepared baking dish. Drizzle with remaining margarine and honey. Bake in preheated oven for 1 hour or until golden and firm in center. Cut into squares. Serve warm or at room temperature

WARTIME
SHEPHERD'S PIE

SERVES 4 TO 6

*In Shetland, we had plenty of lamb, potatoes, and eggs—no need
for ration books. The meat here is expanded with baked beans
and the mashed potato enriched with eggs.*

1 large onion, coarsely chopped

2 tablespoons margarine

1 teaspoon chopped garlic

1 pound ground lamb

1 (8 ounce) can vegetarian baked beans

1 tablespoon steak sauce

salt and pepper to taste

2 eggs, lightly beaten

4 cups cold mashed potato

paprika to sprinkle

Preheat oven to 375°F. In a saucepan, sauté the onion in melted
margarine over medium heat until soft, about 8 minutes. Add the
garlic and lamb and cook until lamb has lost its pinkness. Stir in the
baked beans, steak sauce, and salt and pepper to taste. Transfer to a
deep 10-inch pie dish.

In a separate bowl, add the eggs to the mashed potatoes. Beat to mix
well. Spoon over the meat mixture, roughing up surface with a fork.
Sprinkle with paprika. Bake in preheated oven for 25 to 30 minutes,
or until meat mixture is bubbly. Serve hot.

DUCHESSE POTATOES

For special occasions, Ma gussied up this potato dish, using two spoons to shape it. May also be pressed through a pastry bag fitted with a large star-pipe. For a meat meal, potato water was substituted for milk.

2 pounds potatoes, peeled and cut in 1-inch chunks
1 teaspoon salt
3 tablespoons margarine or butter
1 tablespoon finely chopped chives
1 egg, lightly beaten
2–3 tablespoons milk
salt and white pepper to taste
paprika to sprinkle

Preheat oven to 375°F. Spray a baking sheet with nonstick cooking spray.

Place potatoes in a saucepan. Cover with water and salt. Bring to boil. Cook for 15 minutes, or until potatoes are cooked but not broken down. A knife blade should slide in and out easily. Drain well. Add the margarine and beat until smooth (may also do this with an electric mixer). Beat in the chives, egg, and enough milk to make a stiff mixture. Season to taste with salt and pepper.

Using two tablespoons, shape mixture into egg shapes and place on prepared baking sheet. Sprinkle with paprika. Bake in preheated oven until beginning to brown, about 15 minutes. Serve with meat or fish dishes.

9

The Midnight Mackerel Supper

Flying from Philadelphia to the Shetland Islands with two young-sters in tow was no picnic. But twenty hours later (if there were no de-lays), after making two connections and surviving a white-knuckled landing that skimmed the high, sheer cliffs rising out of the wild Atlantic Ocean, we clambered down a rickety stepladder from the plane onto the tarmac.

The Hofman family had arrived at Sumburgh, the most northerly commercial airport in Britain. In the late 1960s, Sumburgh was a vil-lage of *crofts*, sprawling from the seashore to the rolling hills. My hus-band Walter and I dragged bags bursting with jackets, coats, books, and all the necessities to entertain two small boys on a long journey. Our sons, Andrew and Michael, ran towards the low, white terminal building, where my parents were waiting with open arms. The sight of sheep grazing on heather-covered hills, salty sea breezes, and the waves breaking on the beach just yards away from the airport swept away our exhaustion. We were rejuvenated, united with parents and grandparents, and thrilled to begin our annual Shetland holiday. Hugs, kisses, and a few tears all round. Then, with bodies and luggage safely stashed in the Austin, Dad slid into the driver's seat.

The road into Lerwick winds through spectacular scenery. Purple, rolling hills lie to the west. On the east, islets where the only inhabitants are sheep lie as if suspended on the surface of the mid-night-blue ocean. Battered cliffs are home to thousands of puffins and other birds. In amongst it all, little cottages like matchboxes dot the landscape. The serenity that calms and soothes remains today, and the frenzied hassles, left behind, are soon forgotten.

Andrew and Michael were wide-awake and full of questions. Dad answered with more patience than he ever had with my brothers and me.

"Grandpa, why are you sitting on the wrong side of the car?"

" The steering wheel on British cars is on the left," he explained.

"Why is that?"

"Well, we drive on the left."

"But in America, everybody drives on the right—why is that?"

Dad quickly changed the subject, "Do you know what Grandma has for you?"

They fell for it. Jumping up and down on the back seat, they implored, "Tell us, tell us!"

"Well,"—Dad always prefaced his sentences with a "well"—"first we'll sit in the living room at the big round table and have a plate of soup. Grandma has spent all day cooking for you."

"What else, what else?" Andrew screamed with delight. He liked this game, acted out each year at the beginning of vacation.

"Well, she made the creamy custard you like . . . and if you're very good, she'll give you a Cadbury's Flaky. You know, the chocolate you like to crumble on top."

"What else, tell us, there's more!" They knew full well that hidden somewhere in the house was at least one toy for each.

Dad teased. "This is something very special, but you'll have to wait until we get to Elro, then you'll see. Meantime, look out on the ocean. Do you see Uncle Johnny's fishing boat? He left Hamnavoe this morning for the herring fishing."

This kept them busy until an hour later, when we arrived at Elro, the one-story bungalow built for us in 1946 and named for my brother Roy and me. The silver letters shone brightly on the green picket gate.

Ma's cure for everything, from fatigue to flu, was a bowl of chicken soup, and now that we had finally arrived, soup was essential. Happily, we supped the golden broth and fluffy *matzo* balls.

"This will warm you right to the cockles of your heart!" she assured us.

I still don't know what cockles are, but after the soup, we felt completely at peace. In Elro, there were no problems to be solved, no troubles. Three glorious weeks stretched out before us.

Ma insisted on good manners. "That's how you were brought up," she told me, "and in this house Andrew and Michael will act accordingly."

They learned fast.

"May we leave the table? We want to look for our presents."

"Yes, you may," replied Ma, with a look towards me that said, "See? That's how they should always behave."

"Ma, they do have good manners. They're just so excited at being here, occasionally they might forget."

"Humph," she muttered, turning her attention to Andrew and Michael, who had rushed into the room, almost falling over each other in their excitement.

"Look what I got!" shouted Andrew, holding out a model yacht. At four, he had not yet realized that he could talk at a normal pitch and still be understood.

"Me too!" yelled his younger brother, Michael, plonking the exact model into my lap for inspection.

The boats were perfect and built to scale. In winter, when the days of fishing were few because of bad weather, a talented Whalsay fisherman carved them, each with a varnished wooden hull, sails of buff-colored canvas that could be raised or lowered by a little wooden lever, and a small cabin complete with wheel, compass, and sailor wearing a peaked captain's cap. A coil of thick string was attached to the hull end.

Andrew was impatient, hopping from one foot to the other. "Can we go sail it now? I'll be careful."

"No, we have to do one more thing," said Dad. " We have to name them. What will it be?"

After many suggestions, none of which could be agreed on, Dad settled on the names.

"How about *Maid of the Mist*. That's the boat I used to go on when I traveled to the Fair Isle."

That was fine for Andrew.

"What about my boat?" wailed Michael.

Dad chuckled, "We'll name yours *Mike's Boat*. That's original and you'll always know which is yours."

The rest of the afternoon was taken up with painting the names on both boats with red nail polish, quickly bought from the Medical Hall, the chemist's shop on the corner.

Dad promised. "We'll go to Hamnavoe tomorrow and you can sail *Maid of the Mist* and *Mike's Boat* on the beach. The water is calm there, but," he warned, " you have to hold tight onto the rope so the boats don't sail away and get lost."

We all loved going to Twin Cottage on the island of Hamnavoe, where the Laurensons—Johann, Johnny, and their children—our extended family, lived. The cottage was really two small dwellings, *but and bens* that had been joined together, connected by a narrow passage. Long and low, with gleaming whitewashed walls and a black-tarred roof, Twin Cottage stands in the shadow of the Big Kirk, a church. Even in midsummer, when the temperature rarely exceeds the low sixty-degree range, there was always a fire burning. From the top of the *brae,* wisps of smoke could be seen curling lazily from the chimney pot up towards a clear blue sky. It was, and still is, the prettiest of all the cottages. Each spring, Johann painted the shoulder-high, wrought-iron railings with intricate floral designs—the flowers brilliant yellow, red, and orange, the leaves apple green. In the miniature front garden, flowers bloomed from early summer until late autumn, when frost seemed to rim the moon. The still evening air was filled with the spicy perfume of the flowers: tall pink hollyhocks, brilliant orange double marigolds, and delicate pastel-shaded, night-scented stock. The short pathway from the gate to the door and garden flowerbeds was edged with fluted seashells.

Andrew and Michael ran, unsupervised, over the fields. There was little or no traffic on the one unpaved road, and, anyway, a *crofter* always seemed to be wandering on the beach or over the hills, keeping an eye on sheep. If any trouble arose, help was at hand. My husband, Walter, went to the "herring fishing" with the Laurenson men, who owned their own boat. Depending on weather and the availability of herring, they often stayed out overnight, with Walter "working for his

Twin cottage, Hamnavoe, our summer retreat

Mackerel at Midnight

Johann Laurenson, in Hamnavoe

keep" by helping to haul in the nets. We knew everyone in the small community and had a long list of folk to see. They all welcomed Ma and me with tea and foil-wrapped biscuits, kept for company, and plied us with questions.

"Tell us about America. Is it very hot in summer?"

"What are supermarkets—do they really sell Tampax as well as flour and sugar?"

And to me: "Are you eating enough? You're thin as a beanpole. Jean, you'll have to fatten her up."

No television or movie houses existed, but there were debating societies, concerts in the village hall, and church teas with "home bakes," cakes all baked by local women. The whole community participated in these social events.

During the day, everyone had plenty of chores. Eggs were gathered from the hen house so that we could eat new-laid boiled eggs each morning. With the top cracked off, a knob of butter cut in, and a sprinkling of salt, a fresh egg tasted of wild grasses and marsh marigolds,

Trays of "home bakes" at a fund-raising tea in Cunningsburgh country hall

part of the free-roaming diet of the half-dozen hens. We went to the well to pump cold, crystal-clear water into deep pails. Everyone pitched in to cook and clean except Dad and Uncle Johnny. They sat reminiscing for hours on rocking chairs inside the painted wrought-iron gate, with wisps of milky smoke from their pipes rising into the still air.

"Do you *mind* the time we came up on the boat together?" Johnny said between puffs. "I felt sorry for you all dressed up in breeches and a long coat when the rest of us were in dungarees and *gansies*. But when we began talking, and I could hardly understand you, I felt a kind of kinship."

"It was a long time ago. Surely, nearly forty years past. A lot of water under the bridge since then," Dad mused.

"Man, I never thought you'd stay here."

"Neither did I. But the folk were kind and the place sort of grows on you. Once I got me a wife, I never wanted to leave."

"And she's done well for you. You have *bonnie bairns*, a fine house, and a prosperous shop."

Their bursts of laughter could be heard over the still air.

They talked late into the night until Johann called.

Mackerel at Midnight

"It's time for a cup of tea and bed."

"Lass, I'll have plenty sleep when I'm six feet under," Johnny said, with his typically wry, clever sense of humor.

Memories of holidays in Hamnavoe came flooding back. As a child, I couldn't wait for the summer to begin. The day after school closed, my suitcase was packed. I was ready to go to Hamnavoe—to the wide-open spaces of the island—where I knew the Laurenson family would welcome me. To me, their home, Twin Cottage, meant freedom: no school, bedtime whenever I felt like it, renewed friendships, and so much to explore. Best of all, I had my own bedroom, the bed covered with a pink satin quilt and the window hung with matching curtains—of course, "bought from Greenvald's." The Laurensons were not only our extended family, but, like the other islanders, also good customers. Ma, although she worked with Johann on all the chores, was completely relaxed, saying, "A couple days with Johann is like a five-star hotel" (though I had no idea what a five-star hotel was like).

We knew that the thirty-minute sea-crossing from Scalloway to Hamnavoe was almost over when we passed the Green Holm, a grassy-covered islet inhabited by only a few sheep. The sea was always choppy at that point, but only visitors, "those poor souls from the South," succumbed to seasickness, vomiting into a steel bucket half-hidden under one of the slatted wooden benches. Well before we approached the pier, a young deckhand emptied the bucket, which he "swilled around with sea water to disinfect," according to the instructions of the boat's owner/pilot.

On the occasions when I traveled with Johann, she led us in singing "Rocking in the Cradle of the Deep." Against the roar of the engines and the waves breaking over the hull, I—all the while trying to stay dry—never did hear the exact words. Just as well, as the hymn refers to eventual drowning. Rebe, Charlie, and Jim were my playmates. Long days were filled with sunshine and freedom. Bedtime came only when climbing hills and running over the rocky beaches wore us out. Because we had no movies, television, or computers to amuse us, games sprang from our imagination. A big, white cockleshell was the "bread plate" for a tea set made of shells and smooth stones, on which we laid out afternoon tea atop a flat rock. To us, our bread and jam sandwiches could have been dainty petit fours. We roamed fields carpeted with red and white clover, clambered over seaweed-covered rocks to the lighthouse at the end of the isle, and combed the beach for washed-up "treasures": colored glass balls from fishing nets, dried starfish, and pink curly shells we held to our ears to "hear" the faint sound of waves crashing on the beach. Round pieces of cork, torn from fishermen's nets, we strung on strands of yellow seaweed, then hung them on a line to dry. And on a lucky day, we might come across a bleached, wooden branch, washed onto that treeless shore. Eventually, misshapen and jagged, the branch would find its way into someone's front garden, where it would provide a background for brilliant orange marigolds, purple lupins, and pink hollyhocks. We wrote notes, sealing them in discarded vinegar or lemonade bottles and throwing them out as far as we could into the ocean, in hopes that we would receive messages back from whoever might find them on distant shores. And we often did, though it might be many months later and from another continent. On rainy days, we huddled in our secret meeting-place, an abandoned, upturned fishing boat, its leaky, black hull blistered and flaked. But somehow, we were always within earshot when Johann shouted for us: "*Bairns*, come and get your dinner!"

Dinner was on the table without fail at one o'clock. We washed our hands in the back *scullery*. When we were all seated, Johann led us in a prayer of thanks for the food we were about to eat. Conversation was lively. We had plenty to talk about: among the adults, the location of the fish and where to get the best price for their catch; and among us children, chattering endlessly, where we went, what we found. Each day was an adventure. I always looked forward to meals, though, to quote Johann, I was "a slip of a thing" and could put away quantities of food without worrying about weight gain or cholesterol.

Years later, when the Greenwalds, the Hofmans, and the Laurensons were together at Twin Cottage, days were likewise carefree, unfettered by the constraints of time. Johann's cooking was hearty and tasty. Leftovers, like *stovies*—patties of potatoes, onion, and roast beef—and sausage rolls, were devoured by appetites sharpened by the clean sea air.

"Why not? Everything is fresh from the yard and sea," Johann announced. Soups were thick with potatoes and vegetables, suspended in a tasty broth and simmered with a bit of *reestit mutton*. Our favorite dish was "mince," ground beef sautéed together with plenty of onions in a rich brown gravy, seasoned with Bisto, the beef gravy mix that Ma never used—a holdover from her kosher kitchen days—but that I thought delivered a punch to all of Johann's soups and stews. A huge tureen of fluffy white potatoes, set in the center of the table, helped to sop up the gravy. Before Johann allowed newly dug-up potatoes in the kitchen, she ordered, "Get a bucket of rainwater from the rain barrel and wash off the soil."

High tea was a lighter meal: fresh herring fried in oatmeal; new-laid boiled eggs, the yellow yolks runny and creamy, and always *bannocks* and oatcakes baked fresh daily in the old black stove. There were no cows on the island, so butter was store-bought and milk came from a can. Old habits die hard. Maybe it's nostalgia, but I still prefer my tea with a splash of Carnation milk.

As the sun dipped down toward the horizon, Ma and Johann sat by the open window, knitting, the needles moving quickly to create patterns they had committed to memory. Everyone in Hamnavoe seemed to be related, and half a dozen aunts and cousins had dropped in "to see Jean." She was well liked and entertaining, her conversation spiked with occasional pithy comments.

"My dears, it's near midnight, but I have a taste for a mackerel right out of the sea."

Charlie and John-Raymond, the eldest Laurenson sons, were outside, sitting on upturned barrels, whittling boats from a piece of driftwood. They were bored. All the young girls were in Lerwick, working at the herring stations, and the boys wouldn't set sail until morning.

They jumped up. "Did you say mackerel? The bay is so thick with mackerel the water is black. We'll go get you a *fry*.

"No, no boys, it's late. I can't put you to the bother."

But they were already running down to the shore, with Walter in hot pursuit.

"I'm coming too."

"Me too," yelled Michael, always ready for adventure.

Tossing off shoes and socks and heedless of sea-soaked trousers, they climbed into a little rowboat, moored just a few yards from the shore. Three pairs of hands shoved Michael in like a sack of potatoes.

Charlie handed Walter a fishing line and a dozen hooks. "Just string the line through the top of each hook like this, then drop the line over the side."

"You don't need bait?"

"The shine on the hooks will attract them."

Near midnight, the light was as bright as day, the water so pristine and clear, that schools of mackerel could be seen gliding unsuspectingly towards the hooks floating under the surface.

Walter, accustomed to choosing the right bait for each type of fish, was astonished.

"I can't believe this—just look, there's a mackerel on each hook and I just threw the line and sinker down not two minutes ago."

His companions were unimpressed. "That happens when there's so much fish near the shore. Now, be quick and pull up the line or you'll lose them all."

A loud splash interrupted Walter's concentration. The boat tipped dangerously to one side. Michael had leaned over too far "to see the fish" and had fallen overboard. Laughing hysterically, Charlie and John-Raymond scooped an astonished little boy out of the water and into the boat.

Michael, spluttering and dripping wet, was indignant. "You didn't have to pull me out—I can swim."

"Yes, but we didn't want the fish to nibble on your toes," joked Charlie.

"Go sit at the back of the boat. We're going ashore."

Half a dozen stocky, gray-haired men, long retired from the sea, were seated on a stone wall outside the village shop, talking idly as old men do. The weather was, and still is, a serious topic. In passing, one would get comments such as "fine night, not overmuch wind," or "the wind is rising—the boats won't get out tonight."

Watching the Laurensons drag the boat up onto the beach, one of the men shouted, "Charlie boy, tie it up with a slipknot,"—sound advice culled from five decades of seafaring experience.

The sun was setting as they all trudged up the hill to Twin Cottage. Walter and Charlie carried a box containing three dozen wriggling mackerel.

"Michael, go tell Johann to have plenty of water on the boil and pull up some *tatties* from the yard. We're going to have a feast."

It was an unwritten law that men cleaned the fish and women cooked. At a respectable distance from the back door, the fish were expertly beheaded and gutted.

"Keep the roes and liver. Ethel wants me to make *stap*," shouted Johann through the window, shaking her head at the thought of Ethel's liking for the native dish, originating from frugal years when little was discarded. I adored the traditional Shetland dish of boiled livers mashed with new potatoes. And since not everyone was as enthusiastic about this dish, I could eat my fill. Only when the mackerel had been thoroughly washed under an outside faucet running with cold water, and the innards tossed to seagulls hovering overhead, could the fish be brought into Johann's kitchen. Ma was overjoyed.

"Thank you boys. You've made my day, or will have as soon as we get this all boiled. Now all we need are *tatties* to go with."

The men retired to the living room for a smoke.

In the kitchen, Ma, Johann, and I filled big pots with water and salt. We ran out to the yard and dug up some potatoes. Then it was time to set the table, covered first with a brightly patterned oilcloth.

"I have no idea how many we'll be" said Johann. "Just put out a pile of plates and knives and forks."

Meantime, the mackerel were plunged into boiling, salted water and set to simmer for twenty minutes on the back of the peat-burning stove. Potatoes, peeled and quartered, boiled merrily like happy dancers in a separate pot, and the big, black kettle was filled for tea.

Johann went into the pantry. "Ethel you forgot these," she said, slapping a pound of fresh butter, a basket of *bannocks* snugly wrapped in a clean dishcloth, and a bowl of rhubarb and clove jam onto the table.

As the grandmother clock on the mantelpiece chimed the twelve strokes of midnight, we could see the sun rising, a brilliant orange globe filling the room with the light of a new day, melting out of midnight softness. Minutes later, the sun broke through the mist where the sea meets the sky, and the bright rays bathed the hills and cottages in a golden sheen. Darkness did not exist. Time stood still.

News traveled fast. Aunt Rosie, Uncle Gibbie, and their son Ollie strolled in. "We saw you coming ashore with a good catch. Are you cooking it at this time of night?"

"Come in, come in. Pull up a chair."

Assorted chairs were juggled around the table. In the center rested an enormous platter piled high with boiled mackerel, less than an hour out of the sea and so fresh their tails curled. Spoonfuls of butter melted into a golden stream to trickle over an *ashet*, piled high with hot, fluffy, floury potatoes.

"Dig in," said Johnny, as he helped himself to mackerel and a double portion of potatoes, muttering, " what fools would eat at this time of night?"

Ma answered gleefully, "Well, we're all happy fools then because there's not going to be one crumb left."

Turning to Charlie, John-Raymond, and Walter, she said, "Boys, I must thank you again, for this is truly a night to remember—the night of our marvelous mackerel feast."

Through the years, until she died, Ma always chuckled about

Mackerel supper at midnight, Ma, *second from left*, Johann, *center*, Andrew, *right*

"the night of the mackerel feast." Leaning back in her armchair, savoring the memory, she marveled, "Oh my, wasn't that some supper. My mouth is watering just remembering the taste of the sea in the mackerel and those floury new *tatties* just pulled up from the yard. It was a joy to behold." Then, "We didn't have much, but we overcame the hardships and the good times were cherished."

The mackerel feast at midnight became another jewel in her box of treasured memories.

The discovery of offshore oil in the early 1970's gave Shetland an enormous economic boost. Bridges now linked up islands previously connected only by boat; roads were widened and improved; and the men who gave up fishing and *crofting* in exchange for working on the oil rigs received huge salaries and financial benefits. The population has been increased by "incomers," families who originally came to work for a short time but, attracted by the country living and laid-back lifestyle, have made Shetland their permanent home. Progress has thrust Shetland into the twenty-first century, though the small fishing village of Hamnavoe has changed little in the last fifty years. Twin Cottage, now owned by new people, appears the same, the wrought-iron fence still painted in Johann's colors. At the top of the hill, a score of new houses have been built and two bridges link the island to the Mainland, so that Lerwick is now only a twenty-minute drive from Hamnavoe.

FRESH BOILED
MACKEREL

Send the menfolk out in a rowboat, about five hundred yards into calm Atlantic waters. Arm them with fishing rods, each fastened with a dozen new hooks. While on the boat, split and clean the fresh-caught mackerel, tossing the guts overboard to the seagulls. Drag the boat up onto the beach, well away from rising tides, and bring the mackerel home.

Women will bring a big pot of salted water to a boil. Add the mackerel, making sure the water rises to about 1 inch above the fish. Cover and return to a boil. Reduce to simmer and cook 8 to 10 minutes, or until tails curl and fish flakes are opaque when separated with a knife. Drain. Serve on a platter with a pitcher of melted butter to pour over the mackerel, and salt and pepper to taste.

Note: if Atlantic Ocean and rowboat are unavailable, buy fresh mackerel from a reliable fish store and cook as above.

FLOURY GIRDLE BANNOCKS

MAKES 8

*The griddle, a cast-iron round disc with a handle, is called a
girdle in Shetland. Bannocks may also be baked on a lightly
floured baking sheet in a 400°F oven.*

2 cups all-purpose flour
$1/2$ teaspoon baking soda
$1/2$ teaspoon cream of tartar
pinch salt
$1/2$–$3/4$ cup sour milk or buttermilk

Preheat griddle over medium-high heat. In a bowl, mix the flour,
baking soda, cream of tartar, and salt. Make a well in center of
mixture. Pour in enough sour milk or buttermilk to make a soft
dough.

On a floured board roll dough out into a circle about $1/2$-inch thick.
Cut into 8 wedges. Place on heated griddle. Cook until wedges begin
to rise a little and undersides begin to brown, 3 to 4 minutes. Turn
over and cook 3 to 4 minutes longer. Centers should be dry and
slightly chewy. Serve hot with plenty of sweet butter.

GOLDEN SAUSAGE ROLLS

Johann baked these for Sunday morning breakfast, making her own "from-scratch" pastry the night before. Prepared frozen puff pastry is a quick and excellent substitute.

8 ounces breakfast-sausage meat, all beef
1 teaspoon dried thyme
½ teaspoon fresh ground pepper
1 sheet frozen puff pastry (about 8 ounces), thawed
1 egg, lightly beaten

Preheat oven to 425°F. Spray a baking sheet with nonstick cooking spray.

On a floured board, roll out the pastry to a rectangle about ⅛ inch thick. Cut in half lengthwise. Set aside.

In a small bowl, combine the sausage meat, thyme, and pepper. Divide in half. With floured hands, shape each half into a roll as long as the pastry strips. Place one roll at the edge of one pastry strip. Dampen the other long edge of the pastry with water. Fold pastry over to enclose the meat, pressing edges to seal. Cut in 3-inch lengths and place on the prepared baking sheet. Brush with beaten egg and make 3 small cuts on top of each.

Repeat steps with remaining ingredients. Bake in preheated oven for 20 to 25 minutes, or until pastry is nicely browned and risen and sausage meat is cooked. Serve hot.

Our Ma prepared herring in a score of different ways. In this recipe, fresh, filleted herring is rolled around sliced onion and bay leaves and baked in a lemon-spiked vinegar. Diners should remove bay leaves before eating.

3 large, fresh herring, filleted
1 onion, thinly sliced
salt and pepper
1 cup white vinegar
bay leaves
$\frac{1}{2}$ lemon, thinly sliced

Remove heads and tails from herring. Cut each herring fillet in half, lengthwise. Place a few slices of onion on each. Sprinkle lightly with salt and pepper. Roll up from tail end to head end. Set each roll on end in a casserole large enough to hold rolls tightly together. Combine the vinegar with $\frac{1}{3}$ cup cold water. Pour over the herring. Tuck in a few bay leaves and the sliced lemon.

Cover loosely with foil. Bake in a preheated 375°F oven for 30 minutes, or until fish flakes are opaque when separated with a knife. Serve hot or cold.

SHETLAND STAP

It's almost impossible to buy fish livers in America. Stap dish is not universally appealing, but it's one of my favorite Shetland dishes. Fish livers are rich in Omega-3, and the resulting mixture is creamy and filling.

1 pound haddock fillets
$\frac{1}{2}$ pound fish livers
salt and boiling water
1 medium potato, peeled and cooked (optional)
salt and pepper to taste

Place the haddock in a small saucepan. Cover with boiling water and a teaspoon of salt. Bring to boil. Reduce heat and simmer for 10 minutes, or until fish flakes easily. Drain well.

In a separate pan, place the livers. Cover with boiling water and a teaspoon of salt. Bring to boil. Cook 10 to15 minutes, until livers are opaque all the way through. Drain well.

Mash the haddock and livers together. Add the potato (optional), and mix well. Season to taste with salt and pepper. Serve hot.

BAKED BANANA RICE PUDDING

As kids, we always fought over who would get the golden-brown topping.

1 egg
⅓ cup sugar
2 cups milk
3 cups cooked rice
1 banana, thinly sliced
ground nutmeg
2 tablespoons butter

Preheat oven to 350°F. Spray a 1½-quart baking dish with nonstick cooking spray.

Whisk the egg and sugar in a medium bowl. Add the milk, rice, banana, and a pinch of nutmeg. Stir to mix. Pour into prepared baking dish. Dot with butter and sprinkle lightly with nutmeg. Bake in preheated oven for 45 minutes, stirring occasionally until creamy and set. Serve hot or at room temperature.

ROCK BUNS

If nothing else, you could always be sure of getting one of these fussless cake–cookies tucked onto the saucer with a cup of tea. I substitute mini–chocolate chips to please the grandkids.

1 egg
$\frac{1}{2}$ teaspoon vanilla extract
1 stick (8 tablespoons) unsalted butter or margarine
2 cups self-rising flour, or 2 cups all-purpose flour and 2 teaspoons baking powder
$\frac{1}{4}$ cup sugar
$\frac{1}{2}$ cup dried currants
$\frac{1}{2}$ cup chopped, glazed citrus peel
about $\frac{1}{4}$ cup milk

Preheat oven to 400°F. Spray a baking sheet with nonstick cooking spray.

In a bowl, whisk the egg with vanilla extract. Set aside. In a medium bowl, rub the butter or margarine into the self-rising flour, or all-purpose flour and baking powder, until mixture resembles coarse crumbs. Stir in the sugar, currants, and citrus peel. Make a well in center. Add the egg mixture and enough milk to make a stiff consistency. Start off with 2 tablespoons of milk, and add a little more gradually as needed to make a dough that stands in peaks.

Spoon rough-shaped tablespoons of mixture onto prepared baking sheet. Bake in preheated oven for 15 to 20 minutes, until peaks of buns are beginning to brown and a toothpick inserted in centers comes out clean.

10

The House on Hayfield Road

When my brother Roy was born in 1941, Dad finally heeded Ma's pleas. The family had outgrown 1 Burns Lane. He bid, unsuccessfully, on every house that came up for sale. The bids were closed, but it seemed that someone always came up with a few pounds sterling more. Ma and Dad were depressed. Who or what was working against them?

Ma had her own opinion. "I won't name names, but I know the rotter who wants us foreigners to stay in Burns Lane." To Dad, she fumed, " I'll never forgive that bloody man—and don't you ever bring him to the back shop for a drink." It was Dad's custom in January to bring friends and customers into the back shop for a "nip o' whisky" and a tiny square of fruitcake. For once, Dad complied with Ma's ultimatum.

In 1945, Rab MacMillan, Lerwick's chief of police approached Dad.

"Harry, there are two lots up for sale on Hayfield Road. I'll bid on both. If you're interested, I'll take one lot and you take the other to build on. What do you think?"

Dad stayed calm. He didn't want another disappointment. "I'll have to talk to Jean first."

Needless to say, Ma was jubilant. "Go tonight and tell Rab to go ahead and put in his bid."

In 1946, we moved to our new house on Hayfield Road, one of the first to be built postwar. Open fields surrounded the bungalow. White daisies and pink clover peeped through tall grasses, perfuming the evening air. At the bottom of the road, foam-flecked waves slapped against huge boulders, relics of Stone-Age lava. Midnight black to pearly gray, these enormous rocks create a solid barrier between the ocean and the town. In summer, flirting teenagers gathered to sit on the rocks, dipping toes into the icy Atlantic water.

The house had taken more than a year to complete. Tiles shipped to Shetland arrived broken and needed to be reordered; wood was warped; and one-hundred-mile-an-hour gales reduced the number of workdays. Owing to postwar shortages and escalating labor costs, the blueprint wasn't exactly as my parents had planned. But on moving day, Ma was overjoyed.

"It's just like Paradise," she exclaimed. "The *bairns* can play outside in the fresh air, I can hang the washing on the line in the back yard . . . and I have a garden."

It wasn't long before a rockery bloomed with deep-blue lobelia, yellow primroses, and marigolds, and pink rose bushes climbed the wall outside my bedroom window. Indeed, standing in stark contrast with the gloomy flat above the shop, the bright, airy house had windows all around, so that light poured into every room. The house was located a mile away from the shop on Commercial Street.

Ma voiced her relief to Granny Hunter: "Thank God, it won't be so easy for Harry to interfere with the children. He'll be home for his dinner and that's all during the day."

The MacMillans became close friends as well as the best of neighbors. Their children were inseparable from us Greenwald kids. There were no school buses, so we walked to school together, played after

Elro, house on Hayfield road in winter, Ma in doorway

school, ate in each other's kitchen. Ma and Thelma MacMillan became confidantes. At odd times during the day, they could be seen, striding over the low, cement-block wall dividing the properties. Ma, slipping through the back door, was usually upset and needed to vent—"Is the kettle on? I'm just fair annoyed"—before launching into a tirade against Dad. "That man went out this morning, no breakfast, and not a word to me or the *bairns*. . . . He's just a monster."

Thelma was sympathetic but rational. "Just never heed him. . . . He'll come round."

"That's all very well for you to say," Ma replied. "You don't have to live with him. Thank God, I have friends and a social life." A star of the Drama Group, she was also on the committees of the Eastern Star, SWRI (Scottish Women's Rural Institute), and the Good Companions, an organization that planned activities for the elderly. She was at meetings every night except Friday and Sunday.

My brother, Jack, was born in 1949. "A happy accident," insisted Ma. Ma was now spending a lot of time in the shop, "keeping the money in the family." So Mrs. Wallace, a friend as well as a baby nurse, was hired to take care of Jack. She was a firm believer in fresh air and feedings exactly four hours apart. Rain or shine, she tucked Jack warmly into the carriage and wheeled him out to the side of the house, outside the kitchen window. Before the four hours were up, we could hear him crying piteously. Ignoring him, Mrs. Wallace calmly went about her chores, feeding Jack not a minute before the four hours were up. Fortunately, she stayed only six weeks. Ma took over, feeding on demand.

"Poor wee soul," she crooned. "He's a big baby and needs his food," she soothed, spooning porridge and cream from a bottle of unpasteurized milk into his eager little mouth. Jack has grown into a healthy, active six-footer.

Schooldays were fun, as much socializing as learning. Ma was firm in emphasizing our Jewishness in every way possible. She arranged a meeting with Mr. Swinton, the headmaster. "Ethel must be excused from Scripture classes," she insisted. "You see, we're Jewish and she doesn't need to be learning the New Testament."

"What do you have in mind?"

"I would like her to have art and music classes." There was no problem or discussion. When my group went to Scripture, I went to the music room or art room. "Lucky you," said my classmates with envy.

We dutifully did our homework, listened attentively, and participated in class. But at lunchtime and recess, we rushed into the playground, running, playing, and generally letting off pent-up energies. After school, we walked the mile home. There's always a fresh, stiff breeze blowing in Shetland, so that we arrived at the kitchen door rosy-cheeked and breathless.

Shrugging off our leather satchels, we called, "Ma, where are you?"

"*Bairns*, no need to shout. I'm here. Now wash your hands, and then you can have your snack."

In summer, we snacked on glasses of buttermilk poured from the white-enamel milk pail, a little blue chip knocked out of the lip, revealing the blue underneath. For a treat, we were allowed to choose chocolate cookies wrapped in silver foil from a big tin hidden in the linen closet. But usually, it was a thick wedge of seed cake or a water biscuit from the bakery spread with butter. A double wall of thick cement blocks, kept the back porch between 45 and 48 degrees, so that milk, butter, and perishables could be stored at a cool temperature. Since these items were bought daily, there was no danger of spoilage. In winter, instead of buttermilk, we had steaming mugs of Horlicks or Ovaltine, flavored milk drinks.

We all sat down together for supper at five o'clock. If Dad was late closing the shop, we waited. By 4 o'clock, Ma was eager to start preparing the meal.

"Get the table cleared off and start on your homework." Obediently, we spread out notebooks, a dictionary, and one of the twenty-four volumes of the *Encyclopaedia Brittanica* on the table.

"Turn off the radio. You don't need any distractions," Ma said, clattering dishes, pots, and pans as she worked around us. There was no point in asking her how to spell a word.

Her stock answer: "Look it up in the dictionary. If I tell you, it'll go in one ear and out the other." That's one reason I was first in my class on spelling tests.

Inspired by Ma, who was a voracious reader, we walked up the lane to the library twice a week. Lerwick library was well stocked with reference books, current fiction, and nonfiction. We were in awe of the stern librarian. "You can take out four books," she directed, "and, please, do not fold in the pages." I read each book from cover to cover.

The kitchen was the hub of the house. Today, we would call it the great room. Much of the wall space was taken up with floor-to-ceiling kitchen cupboards, painted apple green, Ma's favorite color.

Ma was delighted. "I've never had so much storage space. Now I can have a linen cupboard, one for all the dishes and my platters, and one for all my baking and soup ingredients." One cupboard held jars of dry ingredients like peas, beans, sugar, and flour. Dishes and serving platters were stacked on the shelves of the second cupboard. On the floor stood storage bins, which were the empty ten-pound *sweetie* tins from the shop. Some were filled with paper goods, like muffin papers, greaseproof paper (similar to wax paper), and brown paper bags; others held cookie cutters and measuring cups and spoons of all sizes. A third cupboard, built around the hot-water heater, was for bed and table linens, stacked tightly on each shelf.

But Ma was not terribly organized. Pages of the weekly newspaper might be scattered all over the floor in front of Ma's chair, and dusty peat dross often marred the cream tiles before the fireplace. To Dad, who was a neat freak, these were major annoyances.

"Why can't you fold the newspaper after you've read it!" he shouted.

Try as she could, Ma just couldn't fold the paper back into its original, clean folds. This led to another outburst, and we fled to our rooms. Soon, I just took for granted that jars of dried peas and lentils might be on the top shelf of the dish cupboard, or a serving platter stuck between a pile of towels in the linen cupboard. I searched until I found what I needed, but Ma alone knew where everything was.

"Bring me some peas and lentils for the soup," she would ask.

"Ma, it's not here," I whined, opening the appropriate cupboard door.

"Try looking in the linen cupboard. I put the jars there to keep them dry."

Indeed, that's where they were—which brings me to the subject of Ma's soups. Her borscht, chicken soup, and schav were superb. Any other soup was a disaster.

"Run down to the butcher and bring back half a pound of boiling beef [chuck]."

She tossed the beef, a few carrots, onions, and a handful of barley into a pot, covered it all with cold water, then brought the concoction to a boil and cooked it for an hour or less, depending on when she needed to serve the meal. We called it "gray soup" and ate it under duress.

Dad complained, "This is terrible! Why don't you stick to borscht and chicken soup? Now, Johann makes a good pot of soup."

"Go to Johann then!" Ma yelled.

But her fish and chips (thick French fries), fried in olive oil, were sublime. Even Dad described them as "ambrosia—a *meichle*."

"I was cooking with olive oil long before it became fashionable," she boasted.

Once a week, Ma cooked up triple batches of fish and chips: "you don't know who'll drop in." And, always, Mrs. MacMillan snuck in from next door, "just for a taste."

I loved to help, following Ma's instructions carefully.

"Whisk the eggs in this dish and pour a cupful of *matzo* meal in another dish," she directed. Meantime, she poured olive oil from a gallon container into a deep heavy pot and set it on the stove to heat. "When it begins to smoke, it's ready."

Together we dipped fresh-caught haddock fillets first in beaten eggs, then in the *matzo* meal. Ma slid the coated fillets gently into the smoking oil, frying them to golden-brown crispness. Perfectly cooked, the snow-white flakes of fish could be separated with the lightest touch of a fork. Ma's chip pot, a deep, heavy pan fitted with a wire basket, was half filled with oil for chips. The chips, hand-cut into long, thick strips from peeled potatoes, were crunchy and golden on the outside, soft and moist inside. Ma kept an eye on me as I peeled the potatoes: "Don't cut away too much of the white part. The vitamins are just under the skin."

We ate all our meals together, sitting around the table. Evenings, after homework, we played board games like Snakes and Ladders or listened to the massive radio that took up most of the counter space next to the sink. But most exciting for me was a visit from Mrs. Forrest. With deep-brown eyes, black hair, and a fondness for scarlet-and-gold-trimmed dresses, she was mysterious and magical. After numerous cups of tea and cake and biscuits served on Ma's three-tier cake stand, Mrs. Forrest was easily persuaded to tell our fortunes from the tea leaves left in our cups. (I made sure there were plenty of leaves in the bottom of my cup, so that she might find it easier to predict my future.)

The "living room" was for company. In the china cabinet, our brass *menorah* and a *kiddush* cup were prominently displayed. Unfortunately, when the wind was from the east, smoke belched down the chimney, so that friends—sneezing, their eyes smarting—fled to the kitchen. There, they sat around the Raeburn stove. Dad kept two buckets filled with coal and peat on the floor nearby. The Raeburn

Dad, keeping home peat fire burning

heated the kitchen, but, more important, as Ma said then, "it bakes the best strudels and cakes, and the kettle is always on the boil."

A pot of tea was brewed at least a dozen times a day. No matter what the hour, when a neighbor or friend dropped in, it was time for a cup. People were in the habit of pushing open the back door, arriving unannounced—the custom of the day. "Come away in. Sit by the fire and we'll have a cup of tea." It was the signal for a half-hour of news and gossip. In the background, the strains of Bach and Beethoven played softly on the radio. After the five o'clock news, Ma always immediately switched to the Third Programme, the classical music station, though we pleaded, unsuccessfully, to hear the "Top Ten" hits on the BBC.

On Saturday evenings, it was usual for half a dozen women friends to take turns hosting the card game whist in their homes. When it was the Greenwalds' turn, I was thrilled to be given the task of serving tea and snacks. "Make sure it's ready by nine o'clock," Ma reminded me.

Ma's friends all had a major sweet tooth. I baked a tray of Millionaire's Shortbread, renamed Death by Ecstasy by my friend

Wilma. To balance it out, Jacob's Cream Crackers, square crackers, were topped with a mound of grated cheddar cheese and thinly sliced tomato. I slipped them under the broiler for a few minutes to melt the cheese. The results were met with unconcealed admiration. "Who would have thought to do that," marveled Mrs. Forrest, "and she's only twelve." I was thrilled. My first culinary success.

In the cold pantry, scores of odd-shaped, recycled jars, filled with pickles, condiments, rhubarb jam, and compotes made over the summer were arranged on shelves installed along three sides. Tall, glass *sweetie* jars, packed with Ma's famous pickled herring, a few bay leaves, and dill floating in the vinegar brine, stood at each end "to balance."

This seasonal pantry gave *tam* and sparkle to winter and spring dishes. In summer, as we gathered the wild rhubarb and berries, the cycle started all over again. Ma never tired of putting up pickles and preserves. "It's worth every minute of my time," she said as she proudly viewed the stacked shelves. "They're good enough to win prizes at the SWRI competitions."

The shop next door to Greenwald's at 161 Commercial Street became vacant. Ma confided, "With all of you in school now, I would like to buy that shop."

Banks in Lerwick never lent money to women, especially to buy property. But Mr. Mackieson, the far-sighted banker at the Clydesdale Bank, had watched Ma for many years, admiring her business acumen. "Too bad Harry never takes her advice," he thought. He was encouraging: "You can have however much you need—I'll write out the note."

Jean Greenwald's Women's Fashions opened for business in 1951, an instant success. Ma's fashion sense was impeccable, and each customer received her personal attention. Coordinated skirts and sweaters, trendy blouses, and silk scarves were sold out the day they came in. Suppliers sent their newest and finest outfits to her store. "If it's not what I want, it goes right back at your expense," she warned. And she wasn't about to take any criticism from anyone. When my brother Roy ventured an opinion, she would angrily remind him, "Don't you tell me what to do. I was in the rag [clothing] trade long before you were born." Whereupon, he shut up.

I graduated from middle school and went on to the Anderson Institute, the college preparatory school. When the bell rang promptly at 3:55 P.M., Greta, Bella, and Winnie, my schoolmates, gathered in the cloakroom, before gossiping on the long walk home.

Greenwald's two shops. *Courtesy of Dennis Coutts, Lerwick*

Bella, *zaftig* senior and self-appointed leader, was hopping around on one foot. We looked at her impatiently. "Do you have to go to the bathroom, or can you wait until we get home?"

"No, no. But listen to this. Our class is helping to plan the Beanfeast," The Beanfeast was the eagerly anticipated, annual high school dance. No one knew the reason for the name, as the event had absolutely nothing to do with beans. Refreshments were egg sandwiches, sticky cakes, and lemonade.

The rest of us were still cynical. "Maybe this year the boys will dance with us instead of standing in a corner like lumps on a log."

Each girl's goal was to be invited to dance every dance, and at the end of the evening to have one of the most popular boys walk her home. For many girls, that just didn't happen.

I was more excited. Ma had become an accomplished seamstress. "I can't find what I want in the shops here, so there's nothing else to do but to make my own," she said. She made sure that I was always dressed "to the nines": coordinated sweaters and skirts, polished shoes, and my curly hair tied with a matching ribbon. I knew that hidden at the back of a drawer in my parents' bedroom was a pattern for a low-necked dress and some red silk fabric sent from my Aunt Sadie in America. I was confident Ma would use it to create a stunning dress, unlike any other. I watched as she laid out fabric on the floor, pinned on the paper pattern, and cut out the design. When the shop was closed for the day and supper dishes were washed and put away, Ma worked at the sewing machine. Finally, the dress was finished. In the mirror, the soft silk crepe swirled just above my ankles; the waist tucked in, and the frilled, modestly low neckline was embroidered with pink silk roses. I was thrilled, and Ma was satisfied. "You look chust lovely," she said, as we hung it carefully on a padded hanger.

Long resigned to living in Shetland herself, Ma was determined that I go to college. I had grown up and gone to school in Shetland. "You must get away from here. I don't want you to live the rest of your life away from a Jewish community." But for me, the thought of leaving and going to a big, unknown city was terrifying.

" Ma, I don't think I want to go away. Couldn't I just stay here and help Dad in the shop?"

Ma was infuriated. She ranted and raved. "How can you say such a thing? You have such a wonderful opportunity to get an education, scholarship and all. Believe me, you can't aspire to anything if you have no education. Do you want to be stuck here like me?"

Dad didn't say anything. On the one hand, he didn't want me to leave, but, on the other, like Ma, he realized that if I stayed in Shetland I would marry and become completely assimilated. "There's no future for a Jewish girl in Shetland," he admitted.

Days went by. My emotions seesawed between wanting to leave and staying. My problem was solved when I was accepted to the Glasgow College of Home Economics, dubbed the "Do" school (as if all we learned was bread making!). Ma went ahead, confidently gathering all the items from a list sent out from the dormitory where I was to live: blankets with my initials, sheets and pillowcases for a single bed, towels, wash cloths, handkerchiefs all to be marked with specially ordered labels. Only the best was acceptable.

"No, Harry, she's not getting those discount towels. I'll get them from J. D. William's catalog."

I hung back but eventually got caught up in her excitement. My trunk was packed. I had a steerage ticket for the boat to take me to Aberdeen; then, on to a train to Glasgow. All my friends were going away to college. Maybe it wouldn't be so bad after all.

I was no match for Ma's strong-mindedness. She insisted on coming to Glasgow "to get you settled." There was no discussion, but, secretly, I was relieved. I was in awe of how skillfully she navigated us through boat, train, taxi, and eventually to the "Do" school dormitory.

"Lass, this is not the first time I've traveled to Glasgow," she said, grasping my arm as we hurriedly jumped into one of the train carriages. My baggage was safely stowed away by the porter.

Ma thrust a one-pound note into his hand. "Make sure our trunk is at the front, and don't bang it around. It's brand new."

Ma stayed three days in Glasgow. Within that time she made sure I had the best room in the dormitory, and introduced herself and me to Miss Worthington, the stately, silver-haired principal. "Ethel has permission to stay with my Jewish friends at the weekend. I'll send you that in writing."

But, most importantly, she arranged a meeting with Rabbi Kenneth Cosgrove at his office in Garnet Hill Synagogue, an impressive building with Romanesque pillars and Byzantine-influenced mosaics and arches. Rabbi Cosgrove had been Senior Jewish Chaplain to the Armed Forces from 1939 to 1945 and had worked with Ma on some of the Holiday services in Shetland during that time. He welcomed us warmly.

"So good to see you at last. What brings you to Glasgow?"

After preliminary chitchat, Ma got down to business.

"I want to make sure that Ethel attends *Shabbat* services each week. You understand, of course, that she must take a bus. Her dormitory is more than two miles from here."

Though some members of the orthodox congregation would frown on taking a bus on *Shabbat*, Rabbi Cosgrove was a progressive thinker.

"We will welcome Ethel," he said, "and I expect her to join my family for *Shabbat* lunch." He also fancied himself as a *shadchen*. "How about my son meeting Ethel this evening and showing her around Glasgow?"

Ma was elated. Time and place were agreed on. I wasn't so thrilled, especially when I glimpsed the pale-faced youth waiting for me at the bus stop. Ma had insisted she go with me on the bus, assuring me, "It's just to make sure you get off at the right stop."

Ma's example and scrutiny had paid off. Not only did I attend *Shabbat* services each week and participate in a study group at the Rabbi's house, where the young students stuck to my side like bees to a honey pot, but also I joined every Jewish society available. I was a member of the Jewish Student's Society, B'nai Kevah, and Young Zionists. I made friends with Glasgow Jewish students who lived at home and who competed to have me stay with them on weekends. At breakfast, I was introduced to bagels and lox. Glasgow bagels were tough and chewy, but the silky lox was cut paper-thin and scented with the light smoke of peat. My social life was booming. There were weekend parties and dances, and late-night suppers, heavy on the cream cakes, when we returned to my weekend friends' homes. College work somehow got done in between.

My best friend was my roommate, Eleanor Tythe, who was a member of the Young Christians and the strict Christian sect, Plymouth Brethren. Together, we went to dances, movies, and, on vacation, hitchhiked to *Loch* Ness. During spring vacation, after we had set up a tent on the banks near Urquahart Castle, a gruff farmer appeared. "The monster crept up the on the grass only yesterday," he informed us. We hastily packed up and spent the night at a nearby bed and breakfast. Eleanor's mother never knew how and by whom she was "led into temptation."

CREAMY EGGS, FRESH SALMON, AND SPRING ONIONS

SERVES 4

This egg dish is soft and creamy, quite unlike scrambled eggs, which tend to be dry and hard when served here. Ma substituted flaked, cooked fresh salmon for the lox, which was unavailable in Shetland, and early "spring" onions (scallions), using the green tops and bulbs.

2 scallions, thinly sliced

2 tablespoons unsalted butter

8 eggs

$\frac{1}{3}$ cup light cream or half and half

$\frac{1}{2}$ teaspoon salt or to taste

$\frac{1}{8}$ teaspoon pepper or to taste

1 cup flaked, cooked salmon

4 slices brown bread, toasted and buttered

In a large skillet, sauté the scallions in melted butter over medium heat until soft, about 4 minutes. In a bowl, whisk the eggs with cream or half and half, salt, and pepper. Pour over the scallions and stir slowly until mixture is creamy. Remove from heat. Stir in the flaked salmon. Spoon over hot, buttered toast. Serve immediately.

HADDOCK FRIED IN
SEASONED MATZO MEAL

Any other white fish, such as sole or tilapia, may be substituted for haddock. Instead of self-rising flour, substitute plain flour plus 1/4 teaspoon baking powder. Chives, which Ma used to flavor savory dishes, grew wild in our yard.

> 4 haddock fillets
> 2 eggs
> $\frac{1}{2}$ cup matzo meal
> 2 tablespoons self-rising flour
> 1 teaspoon salt
> $\frac{1}{2}$ teaspoon white pepper
> oil for frying

Wash haddock and pat dry. Set aside. In a shallow dish, whisk the eggs.

In a separate shallow dish, combine the matzo meal, flour, salt, and pepper. Dip the haddock fillets first in the eggs, then in the matzo-meal mixture. Repeat. Lay the fillets in a single layer on a plate lined with wax paper.

Pour about $\frac{1}{4}$ inch of oil into a large, heavy skillet. Heat over medium heat until a cube of bread browns in 60 seconds. Remove bread cube. Gently lay the fillets in the hot oil. Cook 4 to 5 minutes on each side, or until golden-brown and flakes are opaque when separated with the point of a knife. Drain on paper towels. Serve hot with Wild Chive Mayonnaise.

Wild Chive Mayonnaise: Stir 1 teaspoon finely chopped onion and 1 tablespoon finely snipped chives into $\frac{3}{4}$ cup mayonnaise.

MILLIONAIRE'S
SHORTBREAD

MAKES 40 PIECES

My friend Wilma aptly renamed this rich and supersweet dessert Death by Ecstasy. Cut into small pieces to serve. Freezes well.

CRUST

1 cup self-rising flour

1 cup shredded, unsweetened coconut

1 cup brown sugar, packed

1 stick (4 ounces) butter, melted

FILLING

1 can (14 ounces) condensed milk

1 tablespoon butter

2 tablespoons golden syrup

TOPPING

4 ounces dark chocolate, chopped

1 tablespoon butter

Preheat oven to 350°F. Spray a 9-inch square baking pan with nonstick cooking spray.

For the crust, combine the flour, coconut, brown sugar, and melted butter. Press into the bottom of the prepared baking pan. Bake 15 minutes. Set aside.

To prepare filling: In a small saucepan, stir together the condensed milk, butter, and golden syrup. Heat over low heat for 15 minutes, stirring often, until golden. Do not allow filling to boil. Cool for 3 to 4 minutes, stirring slowly and constantly. Pour over the baked crust. Return pan to oven and bake for 10 minutes. Cool.

For topping: In a small bowl, place the chocolate and butter. Microwave for 2 minutes on High or until chocolate is softened and beginning to melt. Remove and stir to mix. Spread over the filling. Refrigerate to firm up. Cut into small squares to serve.

11

An Island Passover

The countdown began exactly two months before Passover. Ma checked the dates on the *Jewish Echo* calendar, which hung on a rusty nail under the mantelpiece, where matchboxes, letters, and china ornaments were crammed together in no particular order.

The *Jewish Echo*, now defunct, was the weekly Jewish newspaper, published in Glasgow. The calendar was Ma's guide for Holiday dates as well as Sabbath candle-lighting times. By the time of the High Holidays in September, the pages were well thumbed and grease-stained. Since dusk in the north comes later in summer and earlier in winter, Ma adjusted candle-lighting times accordingly, rationalizing thus: "As long as I light candles, God doesn't mind what time it is."

The *Echo* was her only connection to the Glasgow Jewish community. As she scrutinized the births, marriages, and deaths published each week, she could be heard to exclaim, "Oh my, Annie Smith has passed away. We used to go together to the Locarno dances every Saturday night." Or, "Ettie Goldstone has had a baby. . . . That must be Ronnie Goldstone's daughter-in-law."

Planning ahead was essential. Deliveries were unreliable. The steamship *St. Magnus*, carrying supplies from the Scottish mainland, arrived in Shetland only twice a week, on Tuesdays and Fridays. And if the weather was stormy, deliveries could be delayed. Shetland sea captains were highly skilled, but none would risk the North Sea crossing from Aberdeen while fighting one-hundred-mile-an-hour gales. "That would be madness," to quote a feisty captain of the 1930s. Besides dealing with this uncertainty over getting food on time, Ma divided her days between working in the shop and cooking for the family.

Two days before the Holidays, Ma had extra help. There were no freezers, so cooking could not be done very far ahead. Thankfully, in early spring, Shetland weather is cold, so food was stored outside in a meat safe, a wire-mesh box hung high off the ground, or in our un-heated, enclosed back porch

Putting together the Passover order was a family affair and the beginning of weeks of joyful anticipation. "Go fetch a writing pad and pencil," Ma instructed me. Jostling each other to be next to her, we dragged kitchen chairs across the linoleum floor. "I want to sit here."

"No, I was here first"—this from Roy as he was pushed off the chair.

This went on until Ma intervened. "Ethel, you sit on one side and Roy you can sit on the other side."

Pencil in hand, she began to compile the list. At first, it was not very detailed. In the 1940s the only Passover items available for the eight-day holiday were *matzo* meal, *matzos*, and wine. And from 1940 to 1945, food was rationed so that coupons in the ration books were saved for special occasions. Lerwick shops stocked sugar, butter, flour, jams, and other basic necessities. But Michael Morrison's delicatessen in Glasgow, still in existence, carried foods we tasted only on holidays: sharp and tangy, sweet and sour, exotic and exciting.

Ian Morrison remembers, as a teenager, packing the jars to go to Shetland. "Everything had to be wrapped in two or three sheets of newspaper; then each jar was placed in the box, separated by card-board. That way, if one jar broke, the contents wouldn't mess up the remaining jars."

The list became longer as each of us added our favorite "Jewish foods." Ma yearned for pickles and sauerkraut, which she used to buy in Glasgow whenever she needed to, so half a dozen cans of each was the standard order. Dad insisted on two five-pound wursts (salami). As soon as they were unpacked, the long, fat, garlicky sausages were at-tached with wooden clothespins to a line strung across the back porch, which served as a natural refrigerator, the temperature in April rarely exceeding fifty degrees. For a Passover snack, Dad sprinted up the steep wooden stairs leading from the back shop, through the kitchen, to the porch. Pulling a silver penknife from his trouser pocket, he cut off a hunk of wurst and ran back to the shop again, savoring small bites on the way. Customers never complained if, at times, he reeked of gar-lic. And if our supply of olive oil was low, six one-gallon cans were also ordered, Ma never tiring of informing us once more, "I was cooking with olive oil long before it became fashionable."

Finally, there was the *matzo* order—fifteen boxes. "How much can one family eat?" came a call from Michael Morrison before mailing the first of many packages to "the Greenwalds in Shetland." Ma began to explain, "I need a box for Granny Hunter, one for the Laurenson family in Hamnavoe, one for the Mullays who live at the top of the lane . . . ," before the exasperated deli owner finally hung up on Lerwick 269, one of his best customers. Most of the *matzos* were delivered to our Christian neighbors, who anxiously waited for the unleavened bread, symbolic of the exodus of the Jews from Egypt—and, in their eyes, we were indeed the Chosen People.

When I was eight years old, my birthday fell during Passover. Determined that I should not feel deprived, Ma placed a surprise order. Along with the enormous brown-paper-wrapped boxes containing the Passover order, there was a small package. "Open it," said my mother. I tore off the paper, Ma helping with scissors, and I gasped. Inside, framed in a froth of white tissue-paper, nestled a magnificent, layered, chocolate nut cake. It had been packed so carefully that the swirly rosettes of chocolate frosting, each crowned with a toasted hazelnut, had retained their shapes perfectly—miraculously surviving the fourteen-hour ocean journey in the ship's hold. Memory being enhanced by nostalgia, this remains the most glorious birthday cake I have ever had.

We ate fish every day, but meat only occasionally. Like every island household, we stored a barrel of salt herring to carry us over the winter, when the weather was too rough for the fishing boats to go out. We stored our herring in the garage, covering the barrel with a slatted, easily removable wooden lid. It was my job to brave the wind and rain, sprinting from the back door of our house to push open the rickety garage door to "get a *fry*." Of course, that didn't mean the herring would be fried. It is the Shetland expression meaning "enough to feed the family," in our case, a family of five. Ma rinsed and soaked a few herring, as needed, to make pickled herring, chopped herring, and, occasionally, when fresh herring was out of season, to make potted herring (rolled and baked in a vinegar–bay leaf mixture).

One month before Passover, she put up a ten-pound jar of pickled herring. First, the fish was soaked in cold water to leach out the salt. Then, in a single slash with a razor-edged knife, the head and backbone, with all the tiny bones attached, were removed, later to be tossed outside to delighted seagulls. The fillets were cut into bite-sized pieces, then packed into an empty ten-pound glass *sweetie* jar, layered with thick onion slices (after the *sweeties* were sold, there was no further use for the jars, except in our house). Finally, vinegary brine was poured over the fish to cover it completely. Bay leaves, peppercorns, and fronds of dill floating throughout helped give a piquant flavor, which mellowed over the weeks. The lid was tightly screwed on, and the jar set on a shelf high above the jams and jellies in the back porch. The pickled herring was perfectly marinated by Passover. To make chopped herring, Ma drained a couple of handfuls of pickled herring and hacked it on a big wooden board with a broad-bladed *messer*. She mixed in chopped onion and hard cooked eggs before spooning the sharp, savory mixture into a bowl. Good plain food—no apples, sugar, mayonnaise, or preservatives added to mask the taste of homespun ingredients.

Two days before Passover, our kitchen was the scene of frenzied activity: Ma, Granny Hunter, and "the girl," darting around like hens vying for their daily grain feed. Ma directed culinary operations while she mixed and whisked—never measuring. "Keep that stove stoked . . . bring in more buckets of peats . . . top up the kettle; we need more boiling water." Her cohort cooks followed directions explicitly. The Raeburn stove devoured huge quantities of coal and peat to keep up the oven heat. To boil water, needed to scrub all the pots and cooking utensils, they carried water from the cold-water sink to a stout aluminum kettle on the hob.

Before the chicken soup could be started, chickens were plucked of feathers, then singed over a gas flame, to be sure not a scrap of feathers remained. Nothing was wasted, Ma insisting, "Chicken feet have all the flavor." Accordingly, the scaly feet were thoroughly scraped and scalded in boiling water before they were added to the pot, along with an assortment of root vegetables.

Fresh beets—boiled, cooled, and peeled—were grated on the coarse side of a grater to make sweet and sour borscht. Ladled over a chunky potato from a Dunrossness *croft* (where the soil was said to help produce the mealy texture) the ruby-red soup, flecked with soured heavy cream, was my father's favorite meal. He would sit back in his chair, licking his lips, pronouncing it the best—a *meichle*.

Ma's favorite combination for gefilte fish was halibut and hake, delivered to the door by a neighbor fisherman. He had usually gutted them, but Ma had to skin and bone them. "Pull away the oilcloth," she ordered whoever was around, usually me. "Now hold the grinder steady while I clamp it onto the kitchen table." The grinder was ancient, made of heavy cast iron, but Ma handled it with enviable ease as she pressed the fish through the funnel and into the blade.

We always served two varieties of gefilte fish. One big pot contained oval-shaped balls of the chopped-fish mixture, simmered with onion skins; the rest of the mixture was formed into patties and fried in hot olive oil in an enormous black iron skillet. Not just for Passover, fried gefilte fish topped with a dollop of salad cream (Scottish mayonnaise) and eaten at room temperature was a weekly Sabbath dinner.

Instead of the rich buttery cakes usually baked each Friday morning, Passover cakes were feathery sponge cakes, each made with a dozen new-laid eggs, beaten to a foam with a hand whisk. Baked and cooled, the cakes were sprinkled with sugar, then snugly wrapped in greaseproof wax paper; wine biscuits, coconut pyramids, and cinnamon balls were stored in tight-lidded, round, five-pound tins, recycled from Quality Sweet chocolates, another item making up the conglomeration of goods sold in Greenwald's shop. The last of the bottled plums and gooseberries were transformed into sweet compotes and *matzo* fruit puddings.

Everything was stored on shelves in the back porch. Food poisoning was unheard of. In April, the temperature in the unheated porch was rarely more than fifty degrees. The "girl from the country," the maid, did the menial jobs like scrubbing the floor, then laying down newspapers, "to prevent the floor from getting dirty," as Ma ordered. As for eight days of *matzos*, it was no hardship. We slathered each sheet with fresh, salty Shetland butter, then covered it with a thick layer of Ma's homemade, heather-scented, blackcurrant jam.

Although we usually ate all our meals in the kitchen in front of the peat fire, at Passover we dined in the "front room," the parlor, where lace-curtained bay windows overlooked the fields across the one-lane road. The room was large enough to seat family and guests comfortably. The drop-leaf oak table was set with a white lace tablecloth and the best china and glassware (we didn't possess crystal). Our close friends dressed up in their Sunday-best church clothes. Rebe, a few years older than I, arrived in a new black and yellow tartan kilt, her white satin blouse with a frilly collar peeping out under a black velvet jacket. I was insanely jealous and pestered my parents until, the following year, I was given a similar outfit—not quite the same, but I was happy. Children and adults were silent as my father, in his heavy Russian-accented Shetland dialect, recited parts of the *Haggadah*, first in Hebrew, then in English. I repeated the four questions, and my mother explained the symbolism of the foods on the *Seder* plate. Each year, discussions became more animated, as our devout Christian guests added their comments and views, always in a respectful manner.

Our Passover *Seders* continued, even though the peaceful existence of the Shetland community was shattered by the onset of World War II. My parents had an added fear. Norway, only two hundred miles east of the Shetland Islands, was under German occupation. It was obvious from the bold signage above the shop, announcing the name Greenwald, that Jews owned the store. A German invasion would have meant certain death for our family. Fortunately, the islands being well protected, that never happened. With Lerwick's natural harbor a strategic base for naval operations from 1939 until 1945, thousands of troops, including more than three hundred Jewish men and women, were based throughout the islands. They far outnumbered the local community.

In 1941, Ma decided to organize a Passover *Seder* for the Jewish soldiers, knowing our flat could not hold all those who would have come to celebrate with us. "These poor souls must have a *Seder*. If there are too many for our house, then we'll hold it at the camp." This became her annual mission. It took an enormous amount of dedicated planning. She called the Commanding Officer (CO) in Lerwick to explain.

"Could we have a hut for the evening?"

The head of the forces stationed in Shetland knew Ma from coming into the shop, where he was given preferential treatment and often bought items not available in the PX (the soldiers' commissary). He listened to her plans.

"What else can we do to help?"

"Well, for a start, can we use part of your kitchens?" and, she wheedled, "maybe a couple of helpers. You know, we'll be cooking for about three hundred people."

"You just go in and tell the cooks to give you whatever you need. I'll make sure that they work with you."

Ma gave a sigh of relief. "That's one hurdle taken care of. I wasn't sure if he would agree." The military's Nissen hut was at the north end of Commercial Road, on the edge of town, but Ma had an army truck with a driver at her disposal. "Just call when you need it," assured the CO. "He'll be there in five minutes."

Ma spent days on the telephone, calling Glasgow and London for donations.

"Just send it to Jean Greenwald, in care of the Commanding Officer, Shetland Naval Air Station. It'll find me," she said—adding scornfully, after she had hung up, "Ignoramuses. They have no idea where Shetland is."

Boxes of *matzos*, *matzo* meal, pickles, and olive oil arrived. A kosher wine merchant in London agreed to send wine. When the cases were finally unloaded in the camp kitchen, Ma poured a fingerful to taste. She knew good wine. Describing it as "putrid," she ran to the sink, spitting it out. Furious, she immediately called the liquor store. She screamed into the telephone, with Dad shushing her in the background.

"Don't think that because we're in Shetland you can send us inferior wine. This wine is sour . . . it's undrinkable. I will not serve this to the men and women who are fighting for you and your family . . . you should be ashamed!"

A fresh shipment arrived on the next boat, along with a letter of profuse apology.

I had *chutzpah*," she later told us. "But I wasn't asking for myself. These soldiers were away from their homes and giving up their lives to protect us. The least these shopkeepers could do was to donate the Passover wine."

A team of army cooks and women friends worked together to prepare a complete *Seder* meal, with Ma supervising. They cooked up enormous amounts of chicken soup and *knaidlach*, chopped herring and gefilte fish (even in wartime, fish was plentiful), roast chicken and potato *kugels*, sponge cake and dried fruit compotes. These dishes were reminiscent of the *Seder* meal they would have had if they had been able to celebrate with their families.

But most thrilling for the soldiers and for our family was the arrival of Great Britain's Chief Rabbi, Israel Brodie, the day before the first *Seder*. Ma had arranged for him to come to Shetland to conduct Passover services. The rabbi presented her with two leather-bound Holiday prayer books, signed by him, in appreciation of her tireless work on behalf of the Jewish troops stationed in Shetland in World War II. Now newly bound, the books are a family heirloom. For many of the Holidays, rabbis from England and Scotland made the journey to conduct services in the most northerly point of the British Isles. This continued under my mother's direction until 1945, when the war officially ended and troops were demobbed (demobilized). But the friendships lasted for years, many of the men and women returning with their families to see the Greenwalds, who had given them a Jewish home away from home, and to say thank you.

Three thousand miles across the Atlantic in Philadelphia, my Passover table is set with fine china and crystal. An Israeli *Seder* plate, of hand-wrought silver, contains the symbolic foods, and my husband Walter conducts our *Seder* with warmth, compassion, and humor. But the *Seders* that instilled a lasting pride in my heritage and laid the firm foundation for my Jewish identity were held in Lerwick, on the remote Shetland Islands, where the Greenwald family, in the midst of Christian culture, held fast to their faith.

PICKLED HERRING
—MA'S WAY

4 salt herrings from the barrel
2 large Spanish onions, thinly sliced
peppercorns and bay leaves
white vinegar
cold water
1 tablespoon sugar

Soak the herring for at least 12 hours, changing the water several times to get rid of the salt. Remove the heads and tails. Split each fish down the center front and remove bones. Cut each fillet into 4 pieces. Rinse well in cold water. In a large jar with a tight-fitting lid, place a layer of the herring and onions; then scatter a few peppercorns and 2 bay leaves over all. Repeat layers until herring and onions are finished.

In a separate bowl, mix 3 parts vinegar with 1 part cold water. Stir in the sugar. Pour liquid over the herring and onions, to completely cover layers. Cover tightly. Store in a cool, dry place. The herring will be ready to eat in 4 or 5 days.

4 tablespoons margarine, melted
2 1/2 cups coarsely crumbled matzos
2 eggs
1/2 cup finely ground almonds
grated rind and juice of 1 large lemon
1/4 cup sugar
6–8 bottled or canned plums, stones removed
and shredded with shears
3/4 teaspoon ground ginger

Preheat oven to 350°F. Pour 1 tablespoon margarine into a 1-quart baking dish and brush over bottom and sides. Set aside.

Place matzos in a bowl. Cover with warm water and soak 2 to 3 minutes, until softened. Drain into a colander and squeeze as dry as possible, discarding the liquids. Return to bowl. Add the remaining melted margarine, eggs, almonds, lemon rind and juice, sugar, plums, and ginger. Mix well.

Pour into prepared baking dish. Bake in preheated oven for 45 minutes, or until edges are firm and center is barely set. Serve hot or at room temperature.

WHISKY CREAM PARFAIT
WITH STEEPED PRUNES

Ma regaled us with this recipe, obtained in the late 1970's from a chef at Lerwick's Queens Hotel, at a dairy Passover meal.

2 eggs
½ cup sugar
1 teaspoon frozen orange juice concentrate
¼ cup good Scotch whisky
pinch each ground nutmeg and cloves
3 tablespoons butter, melted
3 Earl Grey teabags
1 tablespoon sweet vermouth
8 pitted prunes
1 cup heavy cream
freshly grated nutmeg

At least 2 hours before serving, combine the eggs, sugar, orange juice, Scotch whisky, nutmeg, and cloves in a blender. Whirl for 20 seconds at high speed. With motor at low speed, pour the melted butter in a steady stream through the opening in the cover.

Transfer the mixture to a saucepan. Whisk over medium-high heat until thickened, 3 to 4 minutes. Do not boil. Remove from heat and refrigerate to chill.

To steep the prunes, place Earl Grey teabags in a small microwave bowl. Add 1½ cups boiling water, sweet vermouth, and prunes. Microwave at Low for 3 minutes. Let stand for 10 minutes at room temperature.

When ready to assemble parfait, whip the cream and fold into chilled mixture.

To assemble, place 2 drained prunes in bottom of each of 4 wine or parfait glasses, spoon the whisky custard on top, and dust with freshly grated nutmeg.

CINNAMON BALLS

2 egg whites
$\frac{1}{2}$ cup superfine sugar
2 cups finely ground almonds
4 teaspoons cinnamon, divided
$\frac{1}{2}$ cup confectioners sugar

Preheat oven to 325°F. Spray a baking sheet with nonstick cooking spray.

In a bowl, whisk the egg whites until they peak stiffly. Stir in the sugar, ground almonds, and 3 teaspoons of cinnamon. Mix well so that no white streaks remain. With wet hands, roll into balls about 1 inch in diameter. Bake in preheated oven for 15 to 20 minutes, or until barely firm to the touch. Do not overbake.

In a small bowl, combine the confectioners sugar with remaining cinnamon. Roll balls, while warm, in this mixture. Cool, and roll them again.

12

'Keepin' Cakes for Chanukah

Chanukah, at our house, was always bright and cheerful, even though, in Shetland, darkness falls early, about 2:00 P.M. Outside, streetlamps illuminated frost-rimmed shop windows and cast an eerie glow on half a dozen deserted fishing boats, bobbing on the murky waters of Lerwick harbor.

But indoors, our cozy kitchen was filled with wonderful mouthwatering aromas. I rushed home from school, eager to get into the warm house, where those spicy, sweet, and savory smells wafted towards the front door. There were *latkes,* frying in olive oil spluttering at the sides of the big cast iron skillet; cinnamon sugar ready to sprinkle from a silver sifter; and, warm from the oven, cakes studded with cherries, some with a marzipan topping, coconut pyramids, and cinnamon balls—all set out on wire trays to cool. Ma, her face flushed and a blue butcher's apron tied around her ample waist, stood at the stove, spatula in hand ready to turn those *latkes* at the precise moment when each was crisp and golden. Colored candles had been inserted into my grandmother's brass *menorah*, which was prominently displayed year-round in the china cabinet. At hand was a box of Swan matches, ready to light the candles at dusk. On *Chanukah*, the *menorah* got an extra shine with a soft chamois cloth, although it was polished each Friday morning, along with the tall, rope-design Sabbath candlesticks.

Ma's one and only reference cookbook was *Cooking the Jewish Way,* by Ann Wald, published in 1961. Half a century later, Ma's presence still comes alive within the book's faded purple covers. Stained with splotches of forgotten cake batter, the white pages have faded to golden-brown around the edges, like crisp toast. Some are splattered with decayed traces of often-prepared puddings and pies; other pages have notes penciled in Ma's distinctive, upright handwriting. Once again, I catch a glimpse of the eager enthusiasm and care with which she prepared meals for our family.

I slowly leaf through the pages, as she did countless times, and find cuttings from magazines: pineapple sponge custard, from the *Jewish Echo*; fruit tea loaf, from the back of a package of Great Scot self-rising flour; and snowy apple pudding from *Woman's Own*— recipes she never got around to making or made once and felt "it's not worth the trouble." Dad especially was not very accepting of "fancy food." But at *Chanukah*, when Ma cooked up piles of *latkes*, generously sprinkled with cinnamon sugar, and all the traditional Ashkenazi fried and dairy dishes he adored, he became increasingly mellow.

"Maybe the way to a man's heart is through his stomach," Ma sighed. "At least that's how it is at *Chanukah*."

Ma was never too busy to answer my questions as I leaned, elbows on the table, watching the shreds of potatoes come flying from the hand grater. "Why do we have *latkes* at *Chanukah*?"

I never tired of hearing the *Chanukah* story. I was completely captivated by the brave Maccabees and the miracle of the one-day supply of oil that lasted for eight days. "And that's why we eat foods fried in oil," Ma said, as she lifted dripping *latkes* from the skillet and transferred them to sheets of clean brown paper to drain. We didn't have sour cream or applesauce. "That's all very well for those folks with a delicatessen on their doorstep," she grumbled, adding, "but we're not missing anything. Those folks in Glasgow have never tasted anything like this," Ma said, as she served us from a platter of hot, crisp potato *latkes*, crowned with silky onion rings sautéed in virgin olive oil until they were golden. Another platter held piles of *latkes*, sprinkled with cinnamon sugar, and, on the side, a dish of homemade black currant jam, which Dad liked to spoon over his portion.

Ma was an adventurous cook, who, nowadays, would be called creative. In Shetland, she was "daring." Ma added a pinch of grated nutmeg or ground mace to the cinnamon sugar, "to waken up your taste buds," she said, daring us to voice the slightest dislike. A *Chanukah* meat meal in my grandmother's house consisted of fried salami and eggs—an impossibility in Shetland. However, Ma always looked on the positive side of things. "There's no salami to be bought in this backwater, but we do have plenty of eggs and beef." So, instead, she fried up a batch of sliced beef sausages and sliced onions in a big skillet, whisked a dozen eggs to pour over them, then stirred the mixture all together over a low heat with a well-used wooden spoon as if she were scrambling eggs. For good measure, triangles of brown bread were fried crisply in hot oil and arranged around the mounds of sausages and eggs. For me, this was a close second to a meal of *latkes*.

Each night, the brass *menorah* was lit (the colored candles to fit our *menorah*, unavailable in Lerwick, were ordered from Michael Morrison's delicatessen in Glasgow), we sang "Rock of Ages," and my brothers and I were given Chanukah *gelt* on the first night. We did not get gifts on other nights, but we might have something special at supper—an orange, a bar of chocolate, or a pink sugar mouse. Yes, we did have a Santa Claus decorating the dark fruitcake, and we did hang up our stockings on Christmas Eve. Ma decided, "There's no harm in it. The children know they're Jewish, and a few toys certainly won't make them Christians."

We didn't call it entertaining. "Just come over for your tea," was the usual invitation. Cooking at anytime, whether for family or friends, was "from scratch," using whole, basic ingredients. A fish supper—fried fish and chips from Charlie's Chip Shop down by the Market Cross—came the closest to our modern "take-out." "Vinegar and salt on it?" asked the cook before she dexterously wrapped it in last week's copy of *The Shetland Times*. The fish was moist and flaky, the batter crisp and crunchy.

Convenience foods, processors, and microwave ovens were unheard of. Vegetables, washed under ice-cold running water, needed to be peeled, diced, or shredded by hand. Feather-light puff pastry was diligently dotted with sweet butter or margarine, then turned and rolled the required three times to make flaky layers for fruit puddings or meat rolls. For stick-to-the-ribs steak and kidney puddings, Ma removed the membranes from chunks of suet before dusting them with a bit of flour and chopping them with her *messer* on the scrubbed wooden board.

Even if cake mixes had been available, Ma would never have deigned to use them. When, on a visit to me in America, she was finally persuaded to try a chocolate mix, she wrinkled her nose in disgust. "It has a funny, tinny taste—and it's no wonder, with everything in it dried and fabricated. Anyway, you still have to add eggs, oil, and do the mixing." I was forced to agree, especially when she whipped up a couple of her *Chanukah* butter cakes. The verdict: "no comparison."

As the days shortened into deep winter, housewives compared notes. "What's the best recipe for dark fruitcake?" Every housewife had her own secret recipe. The grocery shops stocked up on dried fruits, ground almonds, and spices, ingredients for the dense whisky-spiked fruitcakes, a traditional necessity for Christmas feasting. Ma made her own version, a moist, yellow cake crammed with dried fruits, which included apricots, golden raisins, and diced, candied citrus peel, steeped in whisky.

At least six weeks before December 25, the yellow fruitcake was prepared and baked. Several pounds of dried golden fruits and glazed cherries were stirred together in a white earthenware bowl. Ma never measured the whisky. "Just splash it over. The fruit will soak it up by tomorrow." Next day, the plump, alcohol-soaked fruits were ready to be folded into butter–sugar batter.

"Use the biggest, strongest wooden spoon and plenty of elbow grease," said Ma, as she furiously whipped the sugar and butter to a fluffy cream with a sturdy wooden spoon. A round, twelve-inch baking tin, dark from years of use, was lined with buttered brown paper, which had been recycled. Ma always saved brown paper bags from groceries or from packages received in the mail. "Germs? Not at all. They're all destroyed with the heat in the oven."

She transferred the mixture, heady with alcohol, to the prepared tin, and with the back of a wooden spoon, pressed a shallow cavity in the center. "That's so that the cake will have a flat top," she explained. And, indeed, it did make for easy decorating when the cake had cooled. After about one and three-quarter hours, Ma carefully opened the oven door and peeped in. A sheet of greaseproof paper, placed over the cake, prevented it from browning. Wrapped in cheesecloth and stored in a tight-lidded tin, the cooled, baked cake only saw the light of day for a weekly injection of whisky, poured in through holes made with a metal skewer.

Ma was firm. "Never skimp on the whisky. Wait until the first pouring is soaked through, then do it again." When the cake was thoroughly matured, a thick layer of marzipan was pressed on top. Of course, the marzipan was homemade: ground almonds, confectioners sugar, egg white, and lemon juice. The cake was finished off with a coating of royal icing, a mixture of egg white and confectioners sugar, roughed up with a fork to resemble snow, before hardening to a rock-like texture. A tiny red Santa Claus, two or three little fir trees, and a frilly paper band around the side completed the decoration. I hated the icing. Furtively, I threw it into the peat bucket, even when I was at someone else's house, before biting into the moist layers, rich with almonds and fruit. One slice of Ma's fruitcake was rich and potent. Guests, salesmen, family—whoever came to the house between Christmas and New Year—were offered a slice of cake and a glass of Crabbie's Green Ginger Wine, before setting off happily for home.

Christmas is a quiet, stay-at-home day for Shetlanders. When I was growing up, the highlight was the Christmas Eve performance of the *Messiah*, which the whole family always attended. New Year's was, and still is, an all-night celebration. Young and old dress up as *guizers* to "first-foot" friends and neighbors, taking care that a dark-haired person is the first to set foot in each house visited (a blonde or fair-haired person is bad luck). The first-footer must also carry in a chunk of peat or coal to ensure that the household will be warm for the next year.

Ma's obligatory Christmas cake, a five-pound behemoth, was served at home and in the shop. A week before Christmas, customers streamed into Greenwald's. We were all pressed into service, mostly to run upstairs to fetch an article that we could never find but Dad could immediately pull out from underneath the piles of trousers, aprons, and towels. A tray was set up in the back shop, with a decanter of syrupy ginger wine, thick slices of Ma's cake arranged on a white paper *d'oyley*, and three or four small whisky *tot* glasses. Offered to favored customers and friends, this refreshment added to the Greenwald shopping experience. Each year, Roy continues baking Ma's recipe, but somehow it never tastes quite the same.

Granny Hunter always joined us for Christmas day dinner, entertaining us with stories of cooking for the gentry, with her aprons always freshly starched and "white as the driven snow." Her contribution to the dinner was a steamed pudding, rich, dark, and fruity. "If you find a sixpenny-bit inside, you'll have a lucky year," she told us. She had wrapped a few silver sixpenny coins in greaseproof paper and stirred them into the batter before cooking. Ma was scornful—"What a *bubbe meise*"—but, nevertheless, when she found a coin, she was ecstatic.

In keeping with the lesser custom of eating dairy foods at *Chanukah*, Ma made "keepin' cakes": light fluffy Coconut Cake, rich in butter and eggs, the recipe calling for desiccated coconut; Cherry Cake, a buttery pound cake studded with glazed cherries; Sultana Cake, heavy with golden raisins; and her favorite, Caraway Seed Cake, fragrant with the little nutty anise-like seeds. As we baked, Ma told us all about how Judith, the brave Jewish widow, fed the enemy general, Holofernes, salty cheese and huge quantities of wine to quench his thirst. When he fell into a drunken stupor, Judith beheaded him and precipitated a Jewish victory.

In the cookbook Ma followed, by Wald, recipe instructions are brief, assuming the homemaker has quite a lot of culinary expertise. Baking was a production taking a good part of the day. Without electric mixers, butter and sugar were creamed to a light fluffiness by hand with a sturdy wooden spoon and a strong arm. Eggs and sugar were whisked with a rotary hand-mixer. A friend of Ma's, an incomer from Aberdeen, was famous for her light sponge cakes. One day, as we were walking to tea, Ma explained, "She beats the egg and sugar with the flat of her hand." I never ate sponge cake in that lady's house again.

We had an electric oven for baking, but, in the country areas and in the other islands, ovens were heated by peat and coal. The cook gauged temperature simply by opening the oven door and cautiously feeling inside with a hand. The more "scientific method" was to sprinkle some flour on a baking pan and note how long it took to brown in the oven. For us children, the best part was licking the spoons and the mixing bowls—the batter, a foretaste of the good things to come.

At *Chanukah*, I go back to baking my mother's recipes. Crunchy, crusted *latkes* and the spicy sweetness of homebaked cakes evoke nostalgic memories, to be shared and treasured.

A SHETLAND
CHRISTMAS CAKE

MAKES A 5-POUND CAKE

Gathering the ingredients for this cake takes more time than mixing it.

CAKE

1 pound golden raisins

$\frac{1}{2}$ pound dark raisins

$\frac{1}{4}$ pound currants

$\frac{1}{2}$ cup dark rum

2 pounds diced, mixed, candied fruits (citron, orange peel, pineapple, red cherries)

$\frac{1}{2}$ pound coarsely chopped nuts (almonds and walnuts)

2 cups all-purpose flour

$1\frac{1}{4}$ teaspoons cinnamon

$\frac{3}{4}$ teaspoon mace

$\frac{1}{2}$ teaspoon baking soda

$\frac{1}{2}$ cup (1 stick) butter, at room temperature

1 cup sugar

1 cup brown sugar

5 large eggs

1 tablespoon milk

$1\frac{1}{4}$ teaspoons almond extract

rum or whisky

8-ounce almond paste

apple jelly

ROYAL ICING

1 pound confectioners sugar

2 egg whites, lightly beaten

1–2 teaspoons lemon juice

Keepin' Cakes for Chanukah

In a large bowl, combine the raisins and currants. Pour the rum over and stir to mix. Cover and let stand at room temperature overnight.

Spray a 10-inch cake pan with nonstick cooking spray. Line the pan with heavy brown paper as follows: Draw an 18-inch circle on the paper and cut it out. Fold paper circle into quarters and snip 1-inch cuts about 1 inch apart around the circular edges. Open the circle and place on bottom of cake pan, with the cut edges coming partially up the sides. Spray bottom and sides again with nonstick cooking spray.

Add the diced, candied fruits and nuts to the raisin mixture and mix well. Add $\frac{1}{2}$ cup flour and toss lightly. In a separate small bowl, sift remaining $1\frac{1}{2}$ cups flour with spices and baking soda. Set aside.

Preheat oven to 275°F. In large bowl of electric mixer beat butter and sugars until pale and fluffy. Beat in 3 eggs, with $\frac{1}{4}$ cup of the flour–spice mixture. Add remaining 2 eggs, milk, and almond extract, beating until thoroughly combined. At low speed, gradually mix in remaining flour–spice mixture. Add the fruit and nut mixture. Mix well with a sturdy wooden spoon or with hands. Mixture will be very stiff. Transfer to prepared cake pan, pressing mixture evenly all around.

Bake in preheated oven $3\frac{1}{4}$ hours, or until a skewer or toothpick inserted in center comes out clean. Cool in pan on a wire rack for at least 45 minutes. Turn out of pan. Cool completely. Wrap in cheesecloth soaked in rum or whisky. Place in a container with a tight-fitting cover and store in a cool place for several weeks. Each week, make a dozen holes on top of cake with a skewer. Pour a tablespoon or so of rum or whisky into each hole. Resoak cheesecloth and wrap cake again.

To decorate: Roll 8-ounce almond paste between sheets of wax paper into a 10-inch circle. Brush top of cake with melted apple jelly. Place almond paste on top, pressing lightly. Spread with Royal Icing and rough up with a fork so it resembles snow. Let harden and store.

Royal Icing: Sift confectioners sugar into a bowl. Make a well in center and add egg whites. Add 1 teaspoon of lemon juice and beat well until smooth. If too stiff, add $\frac{1}{2}$ to 1 teaspoon more of lemon juice. Use as noted above.

CARAWAY SEED CAKE

3/4 cup (1$\frac{1}{2}$ sticks) unsalted butter, softened

3/4 cup sugar

3 eggs

1$\frac{1}{2}$ cups all-purpose flour

1 tablespoon frozen orange juice concentrate, thawed

1$\frac{1}{2}$ teaspoons baking powder

2 tablespoons caraway seeds

Preheat oven to 350°F. Spray a round 1$\frac{1}{2}$-quart ovenproof soufflé dish or 9 x 5 x 3–inch loaf pan with nonstick cooking spray.

In a medium bowl, cream butter and sugar until pale and fluffy. Beat in eggs, one at a time, with a little flour to prevent curdling. Add the orange juice and mix well. Add remaining flour and baking powder, about $\frac{1}{4}$ cup at a time, mixing well after each addition. Stir in the caraway seeds. Turn into prepared cake pan, smoothing top with a spoon.

Bake in preheated oven 45 to 55 minutes, or until a toothpick inserted in center comes out clean. Cool slightly. Loosen edges with a round-bladed knife before turning onto a wire rack to cool completely.

WHITE WHISKIED FRUITCAKE WITH TOASTED MARZIPAN

20 TO 25 SERVINGS

FRUITCAKE

6 ounces (1 1/2 sticks) unsalted butter, at room temperature

3/4 cup sugar

4 eggs

2 cups all-purpose flour

1 1/4 teaspoons baking powder

2 tablespoons ground almonds

2 teaspoons fresh ground pepper

1 1/2 cups currants

1 1/2 cups golden raisins

1 cup chopped walnuts

15 dried apricots, thinly sliced

1/2 cup diced, candied orange peel

1/4 cup whisky, or as desired

TOPPING

2 tablespoons apricot jam, melted

10 ounces prepared marzipan

Preheat oven to 325°F. Line the bottom of a 10-inch springform pan with wax paper. Spray bottom and sides with nonstick cooking spray.

Beat softened butter and sugar in a large bowl until pale and fluffy. Add the eggs, one at a time, with a little of the flour to prevent curdling. Beat well after each addition.

Stir baking powder into remaining flour. Stir flour mixture into the batter gradually, mixing well. Stir in the almonds, pepper, currants, raisins, walnuts, apricots, and orange peel. Batter will be stiff and sticky.

Transfer batter to prepared pan, smoothing the top and making a slight cavity in center with a wooden spoon. Bake 1 1/4 hours, or until a toothpick inserted in center comes out clean.

Let cake cool slightly, about 10 minutes, on a wire rack before removing the sides of the springform pan. While cake is still warm, prick the top all over with a metal skewer. Using a teaspoon, pour in the whisky. Let soak thoroughly. Repeat with more whisky if desired. Cool cake completely before removing the bottom of cake pan. Wrap tightly in plastic wrap and foil. Store in a cool, dry place.

For topping: Turn the cake upside down, so that the surface is flat. Brush the top and sides with melted jam. Set aside. On a lightly sugared surface, roll out the marzipan into a circle large enough to cover the top. Don't worry if some of the marzipan hangs down over the sides. With a metal skewer, score the marzipan into a diamond pattern. Place under a preheated broiler, just until marzipan begins to brown. Watch constantly. This takes only seconds. Cool and wrap as above.

COCONUT CAKE

6 ounces (1 1/2 sticks) unsalted butter, at room temperature

3/4 cup plus 2 tablespoons sugar

3 large eggs

1 1/2 cups all-purpose flour

2 teaspoons fresh lemon juice

1 teaspoon vanilla extract

1 1/4 teaspoons baking powder

1 cup finely shredded coconut

Preheat oven to 350°F. Grease a 7-inch cake pan or 1 1/2-quart soufflé dish with unsalted butter or nonstick cooking spray.

Beat butter and sugar until pale and fluffy. Add the eggs, one at a time along with 1 tablespoon of flour to prevent curdling. Add the lemon juice and vanilla. Beat until mixture is thick and creamy. Fold in remaining flour, baking powder, and coconut.

Transfer to prepared cake pan or soufflé dish. Bake in preheated oven 1 1/4 hours, or until a toothpick when inserted in center comes out clean. Cool on wire rack for 10 minutes before turning out to cool completely. Cut in wedges to serve.

GLACÉ
CHERRY LOAF

½ cup glacé cherries, quartered

2 cups all-purpose flour

1¾ sticks (7 ounces) butter, softened

½ cup sugar

1 teaspoon almond extract

3 eggs

1 teaspoon baking powder

¼ teaspoon ground allspice or nutmeg

Preheat oven to 325°F. Line the bottom of a medium-size loaf pan (8½ x 4½ x 2½–inches) with wax paper. Spray bottom and sides of pan with nonstick cooking spray. Toss the cherries with 2 tablespoons of the flour. Set aside.

In a bowl, beat the butter, sugar, and almond extract until pale and fluffy. Add the eggs, one at a time, along with about ¼ cup of the flour. Mix well. Add the baking powder, allspice or nutmeg, and remaining flour gradually, mixing well to blend. Using a wooden spoon, fold in the cherries. Transfer mixture to prepared loaf pan, smoothing top with a spoon.

Bake in preheated oven for 1 hour, or until risen and golden, and a toothpick comes out clean when inserted in center. Cool completely on a wire rack before slicing with a serrated knife.

13

Spreading Our Wings

Though her heart was breaking, Ma never uttered a negative word when I told her I wanted to go to America.

"I'll never keep you from doing whatever you want—you're a grown woman and there's nothing here for you."

Dad, on the other hand, was indignant. "Can't you find a job in London? America is full of bandits; it's too dangerous."

I had just graduated from the Glasgow College of Home Economics, now a division of Glasgow University. Ma and Dad were not about to pay for me to go to America even if they could have afforded it, but I was determined. Aunt Sadie, my mother's sister, lived in Chicago and wrote affidavits and letters of recommendation. I applied for a visa and passport. To save for the fare across the Atlantic, I taught home economics, English—and whatever else was needed—in two island schools, in Yell and Unst. Another traveling teacher and I shared transportation, a little motorboat, which chugged across the narrow straits in all but the worst gale-force weather.

In Yell, I stayed with Mrs. Black, a jolly, motherly lady, who, on my first day there, cooked me up a hearty breakfast of bacon and eggs, dished up on triangles of fried bread. I had never tasted bacon, but, in order not to offend, I ate a few rashers.

"Do you not like it?" she asked with concern. I explained I did not eat bacon. Next morning, she set before me a big bowl of steaming porridge, sprinkled with a thick layer of brown sugar, two newly laid boiled eggs in delicate china egg-cups, and buttered *bannocks*, still hot from the oven. I ate every crumb, not wanting to risk offending her once more. Thereafter, I would breakfast on *stovies*, porridge, *finnan haddie*—but never again was I served bacon.

In Unst, I stayed in Ordaal House with the Petrie family, where two daughters, also teachers, lived. Mrs. Petrie is the only person I have ever met who could whip up a batch of buttermilk scones while I was shedding coat and scarf and settling myself at the kitchen table.

Weekends were spent in Unst, and the young, unattached female teachers led enviable social lives. One hundred British and American air force men were stationed in a block of Nissen huts, high up on Saxavord Hill, the highest point on the island. Teachers and single women were invited to all their dances and concerts. As the male contingent changed constantly, like butterflies, we easily flitted in and out of romances. No sooner was a battalion of soldiers transferred, than a new batch marched off the troopships anchored in Lerwick harbor. We were young, carefree, and filled with ambition. Marriage was not on the horizon.

In Unst, as in all of the Shetlands of the 1960s, old age was respected and the elderly were cared for at home. Old Hetty lived with her children and grandchildren in Stormy Cottage, a *but and ben* behind the village shop. Winds—which could blow near one hundred miles an hour—could not penetrate the thick, stone walls. Light filtered in through small square windows looking out over the *loch*, the rippled surface sparkling like diamonds in the sunshine, but eerie on dull, rainy days. From the open fire in the center of the room, thick peat smoke drifted upwards through the chimney. A heavy cast iron kettle, filled with sweet, clear well water, hung on a chain over the smoldering fire and was kept just under a boil for the innumerable cups of tea brewed for whoever should drop in. On any evening, Hetty, with a *moorit* shawl over her shoulders and her thin gray hair pulled back in a bun, might be found sitting by the fireside. In old age, she was content, pulling the yarn through gnarled fingers into the pedal-driven spinning wheel and occasionally communing with her long-dead husband, Jamie.

Unst is a mystical island, where supernatural powers are said to be handed down from generation to generation. It was easy to become a believer. I met Hetty when I first arrived in Unst as a traveling teacher. She taught me to spin the wool on an old Shetland spinney, a smaller version of the English spinning wheel. Hetty didn't talk much, but her sixth sense and uncanny ability to connect with the netherworld fascinated me. I was completely entranced. As often as I could, I made my way down the hill, the dry heather bracken scratching my bare legs, to the little cottage. When she realized I was a willing listener, Hetty regaled me with her memories of growing up almost a century before. We were kindred spirits. In a throaty whisper, she told me how the *crofters* had banded together to build the stone cottage, so that she and her husband, Jamie, could have their own place, "adding on a piece here and there when the *bairns* came." Jamie went to the whaling and was away for a year at a time. Besides taking care of the cow, a few hens, and the sheep, Hetty knitted gloves and sweaters with the Fair Isle patterns. "We sent it all to Lerwick and got supplies in return—whatever we needed." No money changed hands. Then there were stories about the little folk, the *trows*, who, she warned, should never be insulted by word or deed.

"They only come out at night—if displeased, they have the power to flatten a corn crop or empty the water pails all over the floor, but those who leave out a jug of home brew or a batch of *bannocks* for the *peerie* folk will prosper."

Needless to say, on many a night, extra food and drink were set out on the paving stones of Stormy Cottage.

In winter, days are short, darkness falls in early afternoon, and dawn breaks late. Electricity had not yet come to the islands, so paraffin lamps were lit to brighten schoolrooms and cottage kitchens. For the most part, people stayed indoors, venturing out only in the evening to visit neighbors, drifting in for a *dram* and a *yarn*, followed often by a *foy*, a night of folk music, singing, and dancing. Everyone in Unst played a musical instrument: the fiddle, piano accordion, guitar, or, in one or two more prosperous homes, the piano. A fiddle hung on the wall, in easy reach, so it could be carried readily from house to house. Evenings at Hetty's started off with sprightly fiddle music and a glass of home brew, ladled from the stone urn stored on a shelf near the fire, the warmth helping to ferment the yeast in what became a very potent drink.

"Tell me how to call on the spirits," I pleaded softly, as we sat by the peat fire, away from the revelry. Hetty did not like loud voices and she had to be in the right mood. If we were lucky, and she "felt their presence," she might cooperate.

"Lass, light the candles and set them on the mantel."

I rushed to light three stubby, white candles with a long taper from a box on the hearthstone. Then, I cleared everything off the small side table, where Hetty kept balls of brown and white yarn, knitting needles attached to a half-finished *jumper*, and a well-thumbed copy of last week's *Shetland Times*. Thin light crept into every corner of the smoke-filled room, wreathing the solid tiger-oak sideboard, table, and chairs all in ghostly shadow. The fiddle music faded and flickering candlelight illuminated Hetty's fragile, bent frame. She had no crystal globe, no Ouija board. Only her fingers, knotted from years of arthritis, rested lightly on the bare wooden table. There was complete silence, but for the occasional lump of peat falling into hot white ash on the hearth. Windows and door were tightly shut and the peat fire glowed red.

The scene was set. Everyone trembled with anticipation, watching her every move. Hetty swayed ever so slowly, back and forth, in her rocking chair, with a white sheepskin thrown over the back. Her eyelids drooped, and her head fell onto her chest as she grasped the chair arms. The rocking quickened, but Hetty sat up, back now straight as a rod. "Is there anybody there?" she called in a surprisingly strong voice.

At that precise moment, a chill wind swept over our faces, lifting our hair; papers shuffled, then swooshed across the room, flying from the dresser shelf to scatter over the floor. Candles flickered, then abruptly were snuffed out, leaving nothing but an impenetrable darkness, blacking out shadowed chairs and sideboard. The only light, a bright halo, quivered above Hetty. As I watched, the table, shrouded in a transparent white mist, slowly rose, inch by inch, above the floor, as though drawn by a magnet towards the sooty ceiling. Hetty shrieked, "I feel his presence!" Violent convulsions shook her frail body, and her chair rocked with an untamed madness. "Tell me, tell me!" Hetty was now sitting upright, stiff as a board. Her lips moved but no sound came out. Suddenly, she slumped forward, knocking over the spinning wheel with a clatter. "Don't touch her," cautioned Ruby, her daughter. I was mesmerized.

Just as suddenly, Hetty pulled herself up. Emotionally drained, smiling weakly, she whispered, "I saw my Jamie. He's waiting for me on the other side and he's so happy." Her husband Jamie had been dead for more than fifteen years.

People may scoff, but, Hetty warned, "These are unbelievers." Whoever was present in the room when she called on the spirits was convinced that something indefinable—an ectoplasm, if you will— hung over us. There is no rational explanation. Afterwards, I needed no persuasion when Davie, the infatuated school cook, who lived in a little cottage at the other side of the dark, windswept *loch*, offered to walk me back along the shingle path to Ordaal House. This was a land where the *trows* might emerge from their hillside caves in the dead of night and spirit folks away, never to be seen again. As Davie pushed open the door, Hetty's warnings followed us: "Watch out for the *peerie*

Mackerel at Midnight

trow, him with evil, black, curled claws and eyes as dark as the devil's blood!" Hand in hand, the wind whistling at our backs, we sped up the hill, through the pale moonlight, until, breathless, we reached the safety of the main road. Looking back, we saw only pinpoints of light marking Hetty's house.

Her séance had shaken me to the core of my being. Those nights, I slept with the hurricane lamp turned up high. But on many a winter evening, drawn to her house like a moth to a flame, I left Ordaal to visit Old Hetty, half-running over scrub and heather twigs to reach the cottage before darkness fell and the *trows* crept out from their lairs behind the rocks. I couldn't wait to experience once again her meetings with the spirits and perhaps learn her secrets—and some I did.

I spent one year in Unst and Yell, receiving "isolation pay" as additional salary for teaching in the outlying islands. I hoarded as much as possible, to save my fare for the transatlantic crossing to America. Teaching in Shetland was a pleasure, both gratifying and rewarding. I recognized talent in many of the children and encouraged them to leave the islands to attend high school and go on to university. Children were eager to learn and parents were supportive. Each day, children were sent off to school with a caution: "Be good and do what the teacher says." That didn't always happen, but at least teachers and parents were in agreement.

Leaving my parents and brothers to sail to America was bittersweet. I was excited and thrilled with the prospect of a new country and a different culture. Dad sent me off with warnings: "Don't ever go on an airplane—it's too dangerous," as he slipped a couple of ten-pound notes into my hand. Ma hugged me and made me promise to "write every week, go to synagogue, and date nice Jewish boys." To comfort them, I vowed, "I'll soon be back. It's only for a year." But as the anchor was raised and ropes untied, and the *St. Ninian* slowly pulled away from Victoria Pier, the sight of Ma and Dad wiping tears away with white linen handkerchiefs—the best in our shop—and my brothers Jack, thirteen, and Roy, eighteen, openly crying, was enough to make me seriously doubt my decision. I fled down the flight of steps to my cabin, threw myself onto the bunk, and wept, determined more than ever to keep my promises to my family.

When the SS *United States* slid into Pier 86 in New York harbor, Aunt Sadie was waiting for me. It had been more than ten years since I had seen her, but we recognized each other immediately. She stood, tall and elegant—dressed in a stylish, black silk suit, with a wide-brimmed, rose-trimmed hat to match—and enveloped me in a bear hug: "Welcome to America!" Once the luggage was loaded into a cab, we were whisked away to the Taft Hotel, where my very first observation was "Aunt Sadie, you can't see the sky." She laughed, "Yes, but the views from the top are spectacular. The whole city is spread out before you. Just wait and see." I was overwhelmed with it all: wide streets jammed with buses and the biggest cars I'd ever seen; masses of people jostling one another and rushing along the sidewalks; department stores with Jewish names like Goldblatt's and Neiman Marcus; and skyscrapers so tall that I had to crane my neck to see the top. More surprises came when we dined. "You've made a mistake," I told the waiter, who had set an enormous salad before me. "I ordered salad for one." "Miss," he replied, "that *is* a salad for one."

The clothes that were stylish in Shetland just wouldn't do in Chicago. Aunt Sadie hid her dismay when I opened my suitcases. Tactfully, she said, "We're in New York. Let's go shopping." Holding up a blue and white dress, I whined, "I made this myself and I have plenty clothes." She was ruthless, discarding it in a pile for the charity Goodwill, along with the rest of my dresses.

I had arrived in a hot September, an Indian summer. Aunt Sadie was firm. "You need transition clothes—lightweight, dark-colored fabrics for fall. " We shopped until we were exhausted, but I was thrilled with my new wardrobe. I had never owned so many clothes: reversible, light wool skirts, slinky sheath dresses, silk and cotton shirts, "and you must have shoes to match," insisted Aunt Sadie, as we rushed from store to store. I was in New York avenue heaven. At last, I blended confidently with the crowd.

Mindful of my promise to Dad not to fly, we traveled to Chicago by train. With white linen and crystal in the gourmet dining car, fluffy white blankets on the bunk bed, and thick towels and perfumed soaps in the toilet of our private sleeping car, this was my first introduction to American luxury travel.

Paper-thin, pale-blue air letters flew back and forth across the Atlantic. My letters were filled with wonder and excitement. Aunt Sadie's apartment on the South Side of Chicago was large, airy, and to me, luxurious. Aunt Sadie corrected me: "It's not opulent. I just have everything to make life comfortable." I wrote home, "It's beastly hot outside but the apartment is cool with air-conditioning and . . . there's a large television set in the living room." It wasn't until twenty years later that television was available in Shetland.

The possibilities for work were wide open. In Chicago, there was no lack of jobs for a home economist. "Take your time," cautioned Aunt Sadie, "there's no rush." She was thrilled to show me the sights and introduce me to her friends, all of whom had eligible sons and daughters, who were to become my friends.

I decided to work at Billings Hospital at the University of Chicago. Mrs. Worthington, the tall, silver-haired director, advised me to do a dietetic internship, "to learn all about American food." At that time, I couldn't tell the difference between eggplant and zucchini. And the portion sizes were monumental, in contrast to what I had been accustomed to in Scotland.

Living with Aunt Sadie was fun, but I wanted to be on my own, nearer to the hospital. "How about if I move into the Nurse's Residence across the Midway," I said one evening.

Aunt Sadie agreed. "I love having you here, but the hospital is just a ten-minute bus ride away" from the Residence.

I worked and made friends during the day, and, in the evening, I dated. Interns and residents were thrilled to show the Scottish Jewish dietitian the sights of Chicago. In summer, there were dinners at the top of the Prudential building and sailing on Lake Michigan; in winter, ice fishing on the lake, skating, and dining by the fireside at suburban restaurants. I couldn't wait for Ma and Dad to come out and visit. There were so many things I knew they would love.

MRS. BLACK'S
STOVIES

*A "stick-to-the-ribs" dish of shredded potatoes, onions, roast beef,
and thick, savory gravy, leftover from Sunday dinner. The
mixture is pressed into melted butter or margarine in a cast
iron skillet. When fried, it resembles an oversized, crispy,
brown pancake.*

2–3 tablespoons butter or margarine
1 onion, thinly sliced
1 baked potato, peeled and shredded
1 cup cooked, shredded roast beef
about $\frac{1}{4}$ cup seasoned gravy to bind
salt and pepper to taste

Heat the butter or margarine in a heavy skillet over medium heat.
Add the onion and cook until softened and golden. Stir in the potato,
beef, and enough gravy to bind mixture together. Press into a round.
Cook over medium-high heat until nicely browned on bottom. Flip
over and cook until underside is crisp and browned. Serve hot.

PERFECT
SOFT-COOKED EGGS

Place 2 eggs in a small saucepan. Add enough cold water to rise at least 1 inch above eggs. Cover and bring to boil over medium-high heat. Remove pan from burner to stop boiling. Let stand 4 to 5 minutes.

Remove eggs from pan and run under cold water. Place each egg in an egg cup, small end down. Slice off the top of egg with knife or egg scissors. Top with a knob of unsalted butter. Sprinkle with salt and pepper to taste. Mash down with a small spoon. Eat and enjoy.

POACHED FINNAN
HADDIE

*Finnan haddie is the market name for smoked, split haddock.
It should be pale gold and moist, with a delicate oak-smoked
flavor. Typically poached in milk and topped with a poached
egg.*

1½ pounds finnan haddie
1 cup milk
½ cup water
white pepper
4 poached eggs
2 teaspoons chopped parsley

Cut the finnan haddie into four portions. Rinse under cold running
water. Place in a saucepan with the milk and water. Sprinkle lightly
with pepper. Cover and bring to a simmer over high heat. Reduce
heat and cook for 10 minutes or until fish flakes separate easily with
a knife. Place on warmed plates and drizzle 1 to 2 tablespoons
cooking liquid over all. Top each serving with a poached egg. Garnish
with a little chopped parsley.

To poach eggs: In an omelet pan, bring 2 to 3 inches of water and 1
teaspoon of vinegar to a boil. Reduce heat to keep water simmering
gently. Break cold eggs, one at a time, into a custard cup. Hold cup
close to the water's surface, and slip egg into the water. Cook until
whites are completely set and yolks are beginning to thicken but are
not hard. Lift out eggs with a slotted spoon. Drain on spoon or on
paper towels. Serve as above.

SALMON SCHNITZEL

On my annual summer visits back to Shetland, Ma upgraded her culinary repertoire with this spin-off version of schnitzel— made with fresh-caught salmon.

1 pound salmon fillet, about 1-inch thick
1 scallion, finely chopped
$\frac{1}{2}$ cup chopped mushrooms
$\frac{1}{4}$ cup chopped parsley
2 teaspoons vinegar
olive oil
salt and pepper to taste

Preheat oven to 400°F. Spray a small baking pan with nonstick cooking spray.

Cut salmon into 4 pieces. With a sharp knife, cut a pocket in each, almost all the way through. Set aside. In a bowl, mix the scallion, mushrooms, parsley, and vinegar. Stuff salmon pockets with the mixture. Place on prepared baking pan, skin-side-up. Brush generously with olive oil. Sprinkle with salt and pepper.

Bake 15 minutes in preheated oven until salmon flakes are opaque when separated and the skin is crisp. May finish off under broiler to crispen skin.

Epilogue

My family's ties were strong, never to be fractured, not even by distance. At college, I always returned home for every Holiday, turning down invitations to fly to exciting locations such as Paris, Rome, and Geneva. In Chicago, I desperately missed my parents and brothers, though not enough to return to Scotland to stay. Airfares were outrageously expensive, but that did not prevent me from taking the long three-plane journey to Shetland each year. As soon as I started work, I set aside part of my salary for the trip and for "emergencies," in case one of my parents became ill.

It wasn't until 1966, and I was happily married, that Dad overcame his fear and agreed to get on a plane with Ma to fly to America, leaving Roy to mind the shop. After the first trip, he was a regular, welcome visitor. He loved going to the market, returning with bushels of peaches, plums, and apricots—fruit that was rarely seen in Lerwick and, when it did appear, was enormously expensive. "Humph," muttered Ma, "this is history repeating . . . what can we do with all this fruit?" And she retreated to the kitchen to boil up big pans of jam and chutneys. I never had to buy preserves or pickles during all the years she visited.

Returning to Shetland, Dad had a wealth of tales to relate to all of his cronies. In Hamnavoe, where my parents were now frequent visitors, Dad and Johnny sat on rocking chairs outside Twin Cottage, long into the twilight, swapping implausible stories. Their peals of laughter echoed out over the clear, still air.

"Well, Harry, you're now a world traveler," joked Johnny, puffing on a clay pipe, occasionally spitting the dark tobacco juice expertly into one of Johann's flowerbeds.

"I *mind* when I was in Canada . . . a grand place for the young." Johnny always regretted that he hadn't insisted on emigrating there with his family. "Johann didn't want to leave her mother," he often lamented.

Dad adored his grandsons, Andrew and Michael, and spent hours reading nursery rhymes to them in the Shetland dialect, spiked with Yiddish. Our vacations "home to Shetland" allowed Andrew and

Michael to run free and play outdoors with no supervision. Dad took them on exciting trips on a ferryboat to Hamnavoe and Unst, where they spent hours at a time playing in a makeshift cart, put together with fish boxes and old bicycle wheels. "Why can't we bring it back to Philadelphia?" they pleaded. Needless to say, toys filled their playroom back in America, and brand-new bikes, complete with training wheels and personalized license plates, were stored in the garage.

I teased Dad. "Dad, you never spent so much time with us when we were little."

"I was too busy making a living," he smiled gently. "Where do you think the money came from to send you to college and buy you dresses?"

"And don't forget your new car every year!" I would joke. That was his one luxury. At the end of World War II, Dad brought the first new car to Shetland—license plate, PS1314.

One early morning, in April 1972, Roy called me. "You better come home—Dad's in the hospital."

In his last years, Dad had carried a small jar of nitroglycerin pills in his pocket, "for when I get a bit of a chest pain," he explained nonchalantly. We worried and urged him to take it easy. But Dad shrugged it all off. He insisted on lifting the shipments of parcels that arrived by boat each week and examining the contents. "I need to make sure that Roy is ordering the right goods—I know what my customers want." It wasn't unusual for him to pack up some items and order one of the staff to take them to the post office to return to the manufacturer. He had stopped driving, but Roy took him to the shop each day. Dad sat on a chair in front of the counter, holding court with friends and customers, who flocked around him. "Can't pass by Greenwald's when Harry is there."

In less than twenty-four hours, I was on a plane bound for Glasgow, with Andy and Mike strapped into seats next to me. The journey, changing planes in Glasgow, was long, especially for two energetic youngsters. Roy and Ma were at Sumburgh airport. On the forty-five-minute drive into Lerwick, Ma immediately took over, transforming Andy and Mike from fussing banshees to wide-eyed angels. Whatever Grandma said, they did gladly.

"My little sweethearts," she soothed. "We'll get to Elro and you'll get the special supper I made for you . . . then we'll go down to the harbor and Jim will take you onto his boat, and maybe, if you're very good, he'll give you a line and you'll go fishing . . . and if you catch a fish, bring it home and you'll help me cook it." And so it went. I was home again.

Roy dropped me off at the hospital, which was just at the other end of the road from Elro. Dad didn't see me as I entered his room. He was sitting peacefully, staring out the window, which overlooked his beloved shoreline. I saw the gentle man he had become—my Dad.

He was wearing his woolen beret and brown-striped, flannel pajamas, the kind sold in Greenwald's shop. Were his thoughts sad or happy? Was he thinking of the years spent in Shetland or the years of hardship long ago in the *shtetls* of Russia? Was he thinking of his wife, Jean, and his children, now grown? He turned and saw me, his face lighting up, the lines round his eyes crinkling with joy and a few tears. "You've come home," he whispered as we embraced. "Where are the *kinder*?"

"They're with Ma. We'll get you dressed. I'm taking you back to Elro."

Now that I was back, I could help Ma take care of Dad. According to Ma, "He has turned night into day and then sleeps all day."

Andy and Mike were enrolled in the school, just a few steps from Elro. In the afternoons, they played with schoolmates, clambering over the rocks and going unaccompanied to the street to buy *sweeties*. For them, the time was carefree and fun, creating lifelong, joyful memories.

In the days that followed, Dad and I sat talking quietly. We had some of our best conversations then, and, yet, looking back, I feel I should have asked so much more.

"I'm ready to leave," he said during one of our conversations. "My affairs are taken care of; I drew up my will with Laurie Peterson. Don't try to keep me when I go."

I sat across from him, holding his hand, and through my tears I promised, "I'll make sure to do what you want."

"Don't cry . . . don't grieve for me. I've had a good life. I'm proud of you and all my children. Maybe Ma and I didn't get along, but I've been happy here in Shetland. Sometimes it was hard, but this is where I was meant to be."

Dad was independent to the end of his almost eighty years. Friends dropped in every evening, and we'd sit in the kitchen around the table. While we had tea and biscuits, Dad stirred the pan of porridge, his late night snack.

On the evening of May 12, Andy and Mike and their new friends were playing in the fields surrounding our house. Mrs. Milliken, a retired nurse and close friend, dropped in, as was the custom. Dad sat down to eat his porridge. "The days are getting longer," Ma observed. "We don't need the electric light on just yet." So we sat in the fading light, talking quietly about nothing in particular.

Dad got up, kissed us all goodnight. "I'm going to bed," he said, as he rinsed his dish in the sink.

Less than ten minutes later, we heard a dull crash. Mrs. Milliken and I ran into the bedroom. Dad was on the floor, unconscious, clad in his pajamas, his clothes neatly folded on the back of the chair. Carefully, we lifted Dad onto the bed, gently covering him with the sheet and blanket. Through my shock, I thought, "how frail and light he is. Dad was always so strong and virile."

All hell broke loose. Ma rushed into the bedroom, screaming hysterically, "Call the doctor! Call the doctor!"

"No, just wait." I ordered. I knew Dad had left us. I was determined to carry out his last wishes.

"Take Ma into the kitchen and give her some whisky," I said to Roy, who was as shaken as I, but did as I asked.

Dad passed on quietly and speedily into another world. Ten minutes later, I told Roy, "Now you can call the doctor. All he has to do is issue a death certificate." And, I added, "Tell him there's no rush." Ma was devastated. They had been married almost forty years. Their life together had become a habit.

"He didn't know how to relax and enjoy himself," she cried through her tears. "It was work, work, work, all the time."

Friends and neighbors rallied round. Davie Swinton arranged for a pine box to be made in accordance with Jewish law. It was delivered the next day. The local funeral home washed the body. Phone calls were made to Glasgow to arrange for a Jewish funeral and transportation of Dad's remains by boat to the Scottish mainland. Our family flew to Aberdeen, then traveled by train to Glasgow. Mrs. MacMillan, our next-door neighbor, went to "the street" and bought my mourning clothes—a lilac sweater, and black skirt and shoes. Ma, whose favorite color was black, had no problem. Her closet was filled with appropriate dresses and coats. Cousin Brenda, living in Glasgow, organized our hotel, cars for the funeral, and the meal at her home after the service at the cemetery where Dad was laid to rest.

It was the end of an era. Friends, neighbors, customers, and acquaintances came to Elro to pay their respects.

"The shop will never be the same."

Ma was confident. "Roy will carry on . . . he'll make it better than before and keep up with the times."

Roy had grand plans. The two buildings that housed the Greenwald shops were completely gutted and connected by a walkway. Three floors were separated into men's wear, women's fashions, and accessories. Bathrooms were installed for customers. Now, Greenwald's had been converted into a department store, the only one on Commercial Street.

The discovery of oil in the North Atlantic, off the Shetlands, brought unimaginable prosperity to the islands. Roads were built to accommodate heavy traffic; bridges connected Burra Isle and other nearby islands to the Mainland; Sumburgh airport was enlarged to accommodate scores of Chinook helicopters, carrying workers to the oil rigs far out into the North Sea. Lured by highly paid jobs on the oilrigs, men and women flocked up to Shetland from England and Scotland. And prior to Roy's selling the shops in 1991, business for Greenwald's exceeded anything Dad could ever have imagined. "Parcels of dungarees and oiled wool sweaters came in and were sent directly to the rigs." Roy remembers, "We didn't have time to open them."

Greenwald's new stores, 1991, renovated by Roy Greenwald

Ma, on phone, advocate for the elderly

Ma became the unofficial spokesperson for the elderly. If Mrs. Mac-quahal couldn't afford coal to keep warm in winter, or the Christmas bonus was going to be cut, Ma was immediately on the phone to the County Council—and she was usually successful in having the problem taken care of.

But with the influx of *Sooth-moothers*, Shetland changed. Strangers strolled along the street, some committing petty crimes, which, until then, were unknown. Chief MacMillan added more police to his force. Doors were locked at night and islanders could no longer leave keys in their cars. The shops on Commercial Street, unable to compete with wages paid by the oil companies, lost staff. Eventually, many of the shops that once made Commercial Street the thriving, main artery of Lerwick life, closed.

Nevertheless, today, Lerwick is still a unique, quaint little town. The handsome granite buildings, which help retain Lerwick's character, are now offices, with gold letters etched on the revolving glass doors. Vestiges of the lively street remain at every step along Commercial Street. Black-and-white mosaic entryways proclaim what was there before: the Medical Hall, Gray's Wine Merchants. And, in Burns Lane, the original foundation stone of the shop that became Greenwald's, marked "built in 1872," is set into the wall.

As always, Shetlanders are warm and friendly. Some, who came up because of the oil, liked the way of life and stayed. They got married and are now a prime force in helping to preserve the precious culture.

This is where I grew up, and I find the habits of the place hard to break. But why would I want to cast aside the family and friends who helped form my character and encouraged me to become the person I am today. So, each year I'm drawn back, like an iron filing pulled towards a magnet, reveling in the peaceful setting—breathtaking sunsets, pristine waters, crystal clear, unpolluted air, and time to talk with Roy and dear friends.

"Keep the family together though you're thousands of miles apart"—Ma's mantra—rings in my ears, as I strive faithfully to carry it out. We telephone, e-mail, and visit, walking in the steps of Harry Greenwald, the young peddler who came from a foreign land and stayed to die in the islands that he loved, and Jean Segal Greenwald, who left Glasgow's vibrant Jewish community to live on an isolated island with a foreign culture. She adapted, and involved herself in island life without casting aside her Jewishness. At the same time, she instilled a long-lasting, Jewish identity in her children.

The Greenwald family is now spread all over the world. But through their trials and hardships, their joys and accomplishments, Jean and Harry Greenwald bequeathed us a rich tapestry. Memories, created over almost a century, whisper of bygone days, of gentler times. It is a precious legacy, interwoven in our hearts and minds, passed on to another generation, never to be forgotten.

Glossary

YIDDISH

bubbe meise: old wives' tale

Chanukah: the eight-day Festival of Lights, which celebrates the victory of Judah Maccabee and his brothers over the Syrian–Greeks in 165 B.C.E. (before the common era)

cheder: Hebrew school

chutzpah: nerve

gelt: money

gonif: con man

Haggadah: the dramatic story of the Exodus of the Jews from Egypt

kashrut: Jewish dietary laws

kichel: crisp cookie

kiddush: blessing

kinder: children

kleine licht: little light

knaidlach: matzo balls, usually in chicken soup

kugel: baked pudding, as of potatoes or noodles

latke: pancake, traditionally made with potatoes, fried in oil

mandelbrot: an oblong, crunchy cookie; Jewish "biscotti"

matzo: unleavened bread, eaten especially at the Passover

meichle: absolutely delicious food

menorah: eight-branch candelabrum, with a ninth branch for the lighter (*shammas*), used at *Chanukah*

meshuga: crazy

messer: wood-handled chopping blade

mezuzah: rolled parchment, inscribed with Biblical verses, inserted in a small case, and attached to the doorpost of a house

nedan: dowry

pareve: neutral dish that can be served with a meat or dairy meal

Seder: a special Passover home service, following a prescribed order, held on the first two nights of Passover; the Seder plate contains small dishes of symbolic foods

Shabbat: the Jewish Sabbath

shadchen: marriage broker

shandig: disgrace

shtetl: little town; small provincial Jewish community in premodern Eastern Europe

tchotchke: trinket

SHETLAND DIALECT

ashet: deep platter, from the French, *assiette*

bairn: child

bannock: soft, floury, flat roll, baked on a griddle or in the oven

biscuit: cookie

bonnie: fair, attractive

brae: hillside

brunnie: molasses and dried-fruit quick bread

but and ben: kitchen and parlor of two-room house

chip: thick-cut French fry

croft, crofter: small farm, farmer

d'oyley: doily

dram: tot, or shot, usually of whisky

fancie: little cake

finnan haddie: smoked haddock

foy: a night of folk music, singing, and dancing

fry: half a dozen, or enough to feed the family and any drop-in guests

gansie: heavy, woolen sweater

guizer: one who wears a disguise, of mask and fancy dress, to withhold identity as long as possible

jumper: sweater

kishie: basket carried on one's back

loch: lake

lodberry: stone house, accessible by boat, often used by smugglers

lum: chimney

mince and tatties: ground beef and potatoes

mind: remember

moorit: dark brown

pandrops: strong peppermint hard candy

pay packet: paycheck

peenie: apron

peerie: little

reestit mutton: salted lamb

scullery: room where dishes are washed

shoogly: shaky

simmer dim: midnight in summer, when daylight lasts almost twenty-four hours

Sooth-moother: one who is not born in Shetland

spurtle: long, slender wooden stick, for stirring porridge

stap: mixture of cooked, flaked fish, mashed potatoes, and fish livers

stovie: crisp pancake of potatoes, onion, shredded roast beef, and seasonings

sweetie: chocolate, candy

tam: good taste

tattie: potato

toff: sophisticate

tot: shot, or small glass of whisky

trow: little supernatural being; as in "troll"

voe: bay

yarn: long conversation, tale